What would you feel if you saw a Muslim in your town? For many, even those in the household of faith, the answer would be anger, fear or loathing—surely not the response Christ would desire. This book, with its provocative title, asks, "How can we build bridges between the followers of Christ and the followers of Islam? Can it be done without Christians having to compromise what they believe?" Written by one who has lived for many years with Muslims in both Africa and Asia, *The Man Next Door Wears a Dress* forces us to examine our stereotypes and at the same time encourages us to explore effective cross-cultural communication. We do have Muslim neighbors. Let us think about the very best ways of loving God and loving our neighbor as ourselves. Béland's work will surely help.

DOUG PRIEST—EXECUTIVE DIRECTOR
CHRISTIAN MISSIONARY FELLOWSHIP INTERNATIONAL

The Man Next Door Wears a Dress is perhaps one of the most relevant and helpful books of our present time for those who want to find meaningful relationships among all peoples. As mankind struggles to find understanding in a world of turmoil, the author explores clearly the heart of core issues that result in either conflict or resolution. Though many authors have analyzed Islam, Christianity, and other religions, the fresh approach of the author comes from knowledge and experience that lead the reader to practical solutions and understanding. This book should find its way into every home and become a classic in the classrooms of all who are seriously seeking ways to see peace established among all peoples. It is written with a fascinating approach to a complex situation in the world today.

ZIDEN NUTT—FOUNDER AND EXECUTIVE DIRECTOR EMERITUS
GOOD NEWS PRODUCTIONS INTERNATIONAL

Before the church can make an inroad into the world of Islam, we have to undergo a conversion within our own minds. We need to stop seeing people as merely Muslims and begin seeing Muslims as people—people very much like us. Raymond Béland helps us to tear down the barriers of misunderstanding, those that unthinkingly condemn all Muslims and those that thoughtlessly glorify Islam, as well as those that we use to glorify ourselves. He shows us that it is best not to denounce another man until, perhaps, you've walked a mile in his dress.

MIKE SWEENEY—PRESIDENT
EMMANUEL SCHOOL OF RELIGION

THE MAN NEXT DOOR WEARS A DRESS

The Man——
Next Door
——*Wears a Dress*

EFFECTIVE
CROSS-CULTURAL
COMMUNICATION

Raymond Béland

VMI PUBLISHERS • SISTERS, OREGON

THE MAN NEXT DOOR WEARS A DRESS

© 2009 Raymond Béland

Published by
VMI Publishers
Sisters, Oregon
www.vmipublishers.com

ISBN: 1–935265–21–0
ISBN: 978–1–935265–21–4

Library of Congress: 2009938344

Printed in the USA

Scriptures taken from the *Holy Bible, New International Version*®, NIV®. Copyright © 1973, 1978, 1984 by Biblica, Inc.™ Used by permission of Zondervan. All rights reserved worldwide.

All quotations from the Qur'an have been taken from The Qur'an, translated by Muhammad Zafrulla Khan, Northampton, MA: Olive Branch Press, 2003.

Cover design by Joe Bailen

ACKNOWLEDGMENTS

I am thankful to the many people without whose help I could never have completed this book:

...my wife, Daena, who has spent months working with me writing and rewriting portions of this book.

...our good friend, H. Eberhard Blanchard and our daughter, Rosaline, who have been very patient with me and spent many precious hours editing my work and making suggestions. The Internet has been a wonderful tool, making it possible to send the documents back and forth across the world to be checked and rechecked.

...my friends who proofread the finished document.

...finally, to God for his help. May this work be used to his glory.

THE PRAYER OF SAINT FRANCIS

O Lord, make me an instrument of Thy Peace!
Where there is hatred, let me sow love;
Where there is injury, pardon;
Where there is discord, harmony
Where there is doubt, faith;
Where there is despair, hope;
Where there is darkness, light, and
Where there is sorrow, joy.
Oh Divine Master, grant that I may not
so much seek to be consoled as to console;
to be understood as to understand; to be loved
as to love; for it is in giving that we receive;
It is in pardoning that we are pardoned;
and it is in dying that we are born to Eternal Life.

"The God who made the world and everything in it is the Lord of heaven and earth and does not live in temples built by hands. And he is not served by human hands, as if he needed anything, because he himself gives all men life and breath and everything else. From one man he made every nation of men, that they should inhabit the whole earth; and he determined the times set for them and the exact places where they should live. God did this so that men would seek him and perhaps reach out for him and find him, though he is not far from each one of us. 'For in him we live and move and have our being'" (Acts 17:24–28a).

CONTENTS

Introduction 11

Chapter 1   Sinful or Culturally Improper? 17

Chapter 2   Saul of Tarsus and Osama bin Laden 25

Chapter 3   Christian or Muslim—Why? 29

Chapter 4   Have You Ever Seriously Considered 35

Changing Religion? If Not, Why Not?

Chapter 5   Why Aren't Moderate Muslims Doing More 43

to Stop Extremists in Their Midst?

Chapter 6   Talk About Being Unfair! 47

Chapter 7   Building Bridges 55

Chapter 8   Sharing with Your Friend 63

Chapter 9   Cultural Blunders 69

Chapter 10   What a Tangled Web! 75

Conclusion 83

Notes 89

Bibliography 91

INTRODUCTION

THEY KEPT CALLING US BABOONS!

A STORY IS TOLD OF AN AMERICAN IN MALI, West Africa, who had two friends visiting from his hometown. The visitors decided to go for a stroll on their own in the capital city, Bamako. As they walked, they were followed by a group of children who kept calling out, "*Toubabou, Toubabou, Toubabou!*" In the Bambara language of Mali, *Toubab* means "foreigner"; *Toubabou* is the plural form of the word. *Toubab* is used to describe any white foreigner, no matter what country he or she is from.

Being followed by children calling out "foreigner!" is a very common thing in Africa. In Kenya, youngsters do the same, shouting "*Muzungu, Muzungu, Muzungu!*" in Swahili. They do not do it to be rude, but rather to catch foreigners' attention and show their pleasure and excitement at seeing them.

On their return, their host asked the two visitors if they had enjoyed their walk. They replied affirmatively, except for very rude children who had followed them calling out, "Two baboons, two baboons, two baboons!" Their lack of understanding of the local language had led these tourists to believe they were being ridiculed when, in fact, it was not at all the case. The children simply wanted to be friendly. Miscommunication!

Tom Krattenmaker's article entitled "How Little We Know About Religion" in the April 30, 2007 edition of *USA Today* takes a look at knowledge of religion in the United States. In his article, Krattenmaker explains that even Christians are poorly acquainted with the Bible and know even less about what other religions teach. He suggests that a better understanding of other religions could avoid future wars. When a person does not fully understand a certain subject, his response to any kind of confrontation can be completely erroneous because the rationale on which he bases his actions may be totally wrong.

The aim of this book is to help you understand the complexity of working and communicating with people of different cultures, particularly Muslims. I do not know as much about other religions, such as Hinduism,

Buddhism, Baha'ism or Judaism, but a lot of what is written here about reaching out to people of different backgrounds should apply to those religions as well.

Much more serious misunderstandings than the one involving the two tourists have resulted in many parts of the world because of a simple lack of understanding of what someone from another culture was trying to say. Tom Krattenmaker is right—a better understanding of other religions and cultures could avoid conflicts in the future. Understanding another religion does not require agreeing with its teachings, but it helps explain why the people who follow that religion react the way they do when confronted by certain circumstances. Religion, in most cases, is intertwined with politics and culture.

His Highness the Aga Khan, spiritual leader of the Shia Ismaili Muslims, when accepting an award at the "Tolerance Awards" ceremony at Germany's Evangelical Academy in Tutzing said the following:

> There is a human impulse it seems—fed by fear—to define "identity" in negative terms. We often determine "who we are"—by determining who we are against. This fragmenting impulse not only separates peoples from one another, it also subdivides communities—and then subdivides the subdivisions. But the human inclination to divisiveness is accompanied, I deeply believe, by a profound human impulse to bridge divisions. And often, the more secure we are in our own identities, the more effective we can be in reaching out to others.[1]

Imagine how you would feel if one day your five-year-old ran into the house blurting out, "Dad! You know the people who just moved in next door? The man wears a dress!" So you walk to the window, look out and see a dark-haired, bearded man wearing a long robe. Indeed, the man next door wears a dress. What would your reaction be? Would it be that of resentment and perhaps fear, or would you see this as an opportunity to build new relationships and learn about a different culture?

Try to read with an open mind. As you read, close your eyes and take time to put yourself into other people's shoes—try to imagine what they think and why they think like they do. What would you think if you were in their place? Would you react differently than they do? This is not a book to be read quickly and be done with, but a book to read and ponder. If a section of this book is particularly challenging to you or conflicts with your viewpoint, stop and reflect on it. You may not be seeing the whole picture. Try to look at the issue with different cultural eyes, seeing beyond only your side of the picture.

Many of our personal conflicts and, on a greater scale, the world's conflicts, stem from our inability to see through the cultural eyes of others. It is a bit as if we tried to play a ball game but none of us played by the same rules. Wouldn't that be total confusion? Try to imagine what a job the referee or umpire would have. Our particular answer to a certain problem or situation will differ from that of people of other cultures because we have a different value system.

As North Americans or Europeans we tend to be task-oriented, while most of the rest of the world is people-oriented. We think that time is important because time is money, but they think that money is not the most important thing—people are what counts. A French Catholic priest, after having worked in Mali for thirty years, said as he was leaving the country, "If I had a million dollars, I would give it just to know what is going on in their heads; to see how they think." After three decades of working and living among Malians and becoming fluent in their language, he still could not understand their logic. I am sure that the Malians could not figure out his logic either, even after all those years.

My hope is that you will enjoy this book, that it will broaden your worldview, that it will help you understand why people of other cultures can be different from you without necessarily being wrong. I have heard North Americans say that people in Britain and former British colonies drive on the "wrong" side of the road. They do not drive on the wrong side of the road; they drive on the opposite side of the road. From personal experience, I know there is really no difference which side of the road you drive on, as long as the car you are driving has the steering wheel on the proper side for the country you are in.

You can imagine what would happen if you went to the UK (or vice versa) and decided that the North American way of driving is superior to the British way and insisted on driving on the "right side" of the road. You would not go very far very fast, and you would continually have to dodge other cars coming at you—you would also have many people mad and yelling at you. Before long you would be arrested. Living overseas with the mindset that your ways are the best will most certainly put you on a collision course with your host country.

World maps made in America tend to have North America at the center of the world, while those printed in Europe have Europe in the center. For a lark, an Australian made a map in which Australia is not only at the center, but in the upper portion, with all other continents placed below the equator. The ancient Roman Empire measured all distances from a point in Rome. A plaque labeled *UMBILICUS URBIS ROMAE* ("navel of the city of Rome") still designates the location in the old city. Everyone tends to view his or her country as the center of the world.

Once when cashing a check in a bank in Ohio, I wrote the date by putting the day first, then the month and the year. The cashier informed me in no uncertain terms that I had written the date the "wrong way." I pointed out to her that it was not the "wrong way," but a different way and that the USA was the only country I know of that writes the date putting the month first, then the day and the year. Even in the USA, the military writes the date putting the day first, followed by the month and year.

The purpose of this book is not to study the roots or the different doctrines of Islam or the rapid expansion of Islam today. It is not to point out what is right or wrong in Islam. This book is to help you see Western culture and Christianity through the eyes of people of a different culture, mainly through Muslim eyes.

If Muslims read this book, my hope is that they will also be able to better understand Christians or, more precisely, those of us from a Western culture and mindset. People from other parts of the world are guilty in the same way as westerners in that they fail to see the other side of the story. Muslims do not want to all be seen as associated with violence, discrimination against women, or intolerance of other religions; likewise, they should not assume all westerners are Christians or have low moral standards, approve of abortion or same sex marriage, etc. Just as many Muslims are Muslim by name only, so are many Christians only nominal Christians.

May this book help you see your own culture in a new light and make you a better communicator with people of cultures different from your own.

Chapter One

SINFUL OR
CULTURALLY IMPROPER?

MY WIFE DAENA AND I have worked among Muslims since 1989, first in West Africa and then in Southeast Asia. There is quite a difference between Muslims in West Africa and those in Southeast Asia, just as there is a difference between Christians in the USA and Christians in Eastern Europe or Africa.

Even though Christians all use the same Bible, denominations, groups and subgroups abound. Take for example the Baptists. How many groups of Baptists are there? I doubt many Baptists themselves would know the answer to that question. There are conservative Presbyterians and liberal Presbyterians. Some Pentecostal groups are mildly charismatic, while others would be considered wild by those who are more reserved. The list could go on. It is quite similar within Islam. There are some distinct groups that we hear about more often, like the Shiites, the Sunnis, the Wahhabis and the Sufis, but there are many subgroups among these. The differences between some of these groups are numerous and significant enough that some of them do not even consider the others Muslims. Please keep this in mind as you continue reading.

What Christians believe and how they interpret the Bible, or Muslims the Qur'an, is in many ways influenced by their cultural backgrounds. Depending on how they were raised, some things might be considered acceptable or unacceptable and it could be the opposite in a different culture. I believe some things can be sinful in one culture, but not in another, depending on how they are viewed through our cultural eyes.

Let me give some examples. In many parts of Africa, women think nothing of showing their breasts in public. After all, a woman's breasts were not given for a sexual purpose, but to feed a baby. It is not at all uncommon to walk into a courtyard in Africa, including the courtyard of a Christian or Muslim, and find women and teenage girls working at their tasks topless. In deference to a foreigner, they might go in and put on a blouse, but not always.

If this would be the case in North America, it would be considered indecent exposure and unacceptable—and, in my opinion, sinful. But in the African context it is not considered sinful because of the cultural differences. In North America, any of us would be shocked if we pulled into the driveway of our fellow church member and found his wife and teenage daughters topless in the backyard, preparing the BBQ.

Paul talks along these lines in Romans 14:5–6, 1 Corinthians 8, and in his epistle to the Galatians. In 1 Corinthians 11:2–16 Paul talks about "propriety in worship." He tells us that women should have their heads covered and be silent in church. Most churches do not follow that rule anymore. They get around the requirement by saying that it was a cultural thing of that place and time. The Jews had their own culture with requirements like not eating pork or not having graven images, but those things were not considered sinful by the Greeks or the Romans. Do not take me wrong—I am not talking about conduct that is clearly marked as sinful in the Scriptures like immorality, murder, lust, or lying. Again, we could write an entire book about how we define lust, lying, or immorality according to different cultural norms, but this is not my goal in this book.

Where we worked in West Africa, it was considered wrong and sinful for a woman to wear slacks or to show her legs above the ankles. In most parts of Africa, it is considered improper for a man to show any sign of affection to his wife in public. Even for a man to hold his wife's hand in public is considered wrong. One Mother's Day, my wife and I were in a large church in Nairobi, Kenya. The pastor was Welsh and had lived in Canada. His sermon on that day was about loving and paying respect to our wives and mothers according to the Scriptures. After finishing his sermon, he called his wife to the platform and gave her a peck on the cheek.

A rustle of surprise went through the congregation and immediately, the elders of that church sent him a note asking him to leave the platform. His ministry in that church ended not long after. In their cultural eyes, it was almost as bad as if he had committed a sexual act in front of the congregation. I could list other such examples.

In a similar way, there are Muslims who believe strongly that girls and women should wear a large scarf covering their hair and neck (in some places called *hijab*), and others believe that a headscarf is not sufficient. They believe that girls and women should be covered from head to foot by wearing various types of loose garments (sometimes called *burka*), leaving only a small slit for the eyes or covering the face with a thin cloth mesh that the woman can see through.

Among some Muslims, women are not allowed to touch a man, even to shake hands, unless he is her husband or an immediate family member. As I am writing this, a serious debate is going on in Turkey over the right to wear a head cover in schools and government buildings. A primary school teacher lost her job for wearing a headscarf on school grounds. At the same time, in many parts of Indonesia, Muslims are trying to pass laws that would make it compulsory for a girl or a woman to wear a head cover in government buildings, schools, etc. It is already law in some parts of Indonesia. The people of both countries are serious Muslims, but from different cultural backgrounds.

As these few examples illustrate, not all Christians or Muslims are the same nor do all subgroups within these religions believe exactly the same way. For both Muslims and Christians, our cultural backgrounds can influence the way we read and interpret our holy books. Christians have debated and fought about doctrinal points and interpretations of Bible passages for centuries, as have Muslims about the Qur'an and other Islamic writings, such as the Hadith. In my opinion, this is in part due to the differences in culture and upbringing.

I am French Canadian and my wife is American. We have found over the years that we have a lot of differences because of our varied cultures and upbringing. For example, in Quebec when I was growing up we never ate fruit salad at the same time as a steak, but Americans did. Fruit salad was considered a dessert. My mother was shocked the first time she saw English-speaking kids eating peanut butter and jelly sandwiches. French Canadians did not do that, and to her it was most ridiculous. But many of my American friends considered peanut butter and jelly sandwiches manna from heaven.

In my more than twenty-five years in Africa and Asia, I have attended many churches, and I would say that nearly all of them were modeled after European or North American churches. The way the people dressed for the services, the way those services were conducted, even many times the design of the buildings themselves—everything was a carbon copy of what the missionaries had been accustomed to in their home countries.

I have to admit that at times, the carbon copy might have been somewhat blurred, but nevertheless, it was modeled not on the cultural ways of the local people, but of the foreigners. No matter how we try to avoid it, we carry our cultural baggage with us.

I do not mean to say that our culture is inferior to others, but at the same time, our culture is not necessarily superior. In his book *Living Overseas*,[2] Ted Ward says there is no such thing as an uncivilized people. Everyone is civilized according to his or her own culture. You know how to function in your own environment; you know what is considered proper and what is not. In the same way, no matter how much a culture may be considered primitive, the people from that culture know the proper etiquette for their everyday activities.

In many parts of the world, people eat their food without using silverware. In Mali, for example, most people eat with their fingers (using the right hand only) from one large bowl placed on the floor with everyone sitting on low stools around it. They do not serve people individually on plates as is done in North America. To them, eating all from the same bowl is a symbol of unity, showing the family as one.

In a Malian Muslim family, if one member becomes a Christian, often the rest of the family will refuse to let him or her eat out of the common bowl and they will serve that person from a separate dish. This is to show them they are not part of the family any longer and therefore cannot put their hand in the food bowl with the others. To put it in a Western cultural context, it is almost as if you were visiting a family and while they sat at the table to enjoy their meal, they served your food in the dog's dish for you to eat by yourself in a corner on the floor.

To the Malians, eating with their fingers from a common bowl is perfectly normal and has an important cultural significance. So, what is more "correct" or "spiritual"—eating with your fingers, or with silverware, or with chopsticks like the Chinese? Each one has his preferences, and although eating with silverware from separate plates is probably more hygienic than everyone eating with their fingers out of the common bowl, it is not more "correct" or more "spiritual." It is just that eating with silverware is culturally "proper" for North Americans and Europeans.

Now, imagine a Malian coming to this country as a missionary and starting a new church in your neighborhood. You are interested in what he has to say about God, but he teaches that Christians should eat with their fingers out of one common bowl as a symbol of Christian unity since Christians are one large family. What would you think? After all, Jesus, at the Last Supper, when asked who would betray him, replied, "The one who has dipped his hand into the bowl with me will betray me" (Matthew 26:23). This would seem to imply that they all dipped from the same bowl. Perhaps it was like a fondue or dipping corn chips in salsa. Leonardo da Vinci's depiction of the Last Supper is most probably not entirely accurate. Jesus and the twelve were not likely to be all sitting on one side of a long table, but rather sitting in a circle on low stools, or reclining on pillows.

For the Malian, due to his cultural background, the way the family eats has great importance, but I presume that you would be reluctant to join a church where they teach that eating with your fingers is more spiritual than eating with silverware, and therefore obligatory. This particular cultural teaching of this well-intentioned Malian missionary might turn you away from his church or ministry.

I am afraid that Christian missionaries have been guilty of doing the very same thing when they have gone overseas to teach about God and his salvation plan. They have brought their culture with them and imposed rules on the people that were not scriptural but simply cultural. In so doing, they have turned people away from the gospel and slowed the expansion of God's kingdom. They, perhaps unknowingly, have imposed their assumed superior culture on the people they were trying to bring to the knowledge of God's salvation. They never stopped to think about the fact that some of what they taught was not in scripture, but they assumed it was there because they interpreted the Bible with their culturally prejudiced eyes.

Some churches say that people should try to imitate the pattern of the early church in the New Testament as much as possible. I doubt that a church service in the days of Peter and Paul looked anything like a church service in the West today. A person would think the apostles had written a book entitled *How Church Services Should Be Conducted.*

We have visited many churches, both in North America and Europe. Except for a few minor differences, most of the church services went pretty much the same way: Someone welcomes the congregation, three or four songs are sung, then there might be a time for testimonies, followed by announcements, the offering, then the sermon. The main differences between church services are that some sing using a song book, others a projector; some clap and raise theirs hands, others don't; some take communion every Sunday, some once a month or once a year; some take communion before the sermon, others after…

God has given us freedom in how a church service should be held as long as it is done in an orderly manner, as Paul explained in his letters to the Corinthians. Being different people, we have different tastes and preferences. An Asian proverb says "ten men, ten minds." Some people like lively music, some like quiet music. One may not be better or more spiritual than the other; they are just different and more or less appreciated according to our preferences. Some people may be very reserved in their expressions of praise and worship, others rather wild.

In North America, most African-American churches prefer more lively singing. They like to "swing" as they sing. It is their cultural way of expressing joy and adoration. Being more reserved and self-conscious, I do not "swing" much, but I do enjoy attending a lively service and seeing the joy and freedom expressed in their singing.

In some churches, it seems as if people sing with their mouths closed, like a ventriloquist. They sing about joy, but look far from happy. What I am trying to say is that one style is not necessarily more spiritual than the other; they are just different. We all have different ways of expressing ourselves according to our background and upbringing.

Christians should try to imitate the New Testament church as they see it in the Bible—more in accordance with its teaching about Christian living than in its style of worship. Many teachings of the New Testament on the subject of divorce, morality, respect for our parents, etc. are being ignored or openly rejected by many churches and believers. At the same time Christians divide on issues like what style of music they should use, should they use one cup or many cups to serve communion, should they be post-millennial or pre-millennial. It is like Jesus said in Matthew 23:24, "You blind guides! You strain out a gnat but swallow a camel."

Teaching in a different culture should be done in a loving and gentle way as Paul said in Romans 14:19–22:

> Let us therefore make every effort to do what leads to peace and to mutual edification. Do not destroy the work of God for the sake of food. All food is clean, but it is wrong for a man to eat anything that causes someone else to stumble. It is better not to eat meat or drink wine or do anything else that will cause your brother to fall. So whatever you believe about these things keep between yourself and God. Blessed is the man who does not condemn himself by what he approves.

Chapter Two

Saul of Tarsus
and
Osama Bin Laden

MOST OF US ARE FAMILIAR with John 3:16. It is probably the Bible verse most often taught in Sunday school. "For God so loved the world that he gave his one and only Son, that whoever believes in him shall not perish but have eternal life." The words "world" and "whoever" *do* include Muslims, no matter how nasty non-Muslims may think some Muslims are.

This book will be mostly about Muslim/Christian relations. But before I go any further, I want to make it clear that my intention is not to condone the actions of Muslim extremists (just as, even though a Christian myself, I do not approve of all the things done in the name of Christianity) nor to approve or reject the teachings of the Qur'an. The Qur'an has a lot of good teachings, but it falls short of recognizing Jesus Christ (*Isa Al-Masih* in Arabic) as our Lord and Savior.

Muslims believe more in a hope of salvation by works (mainly by observing the Five Pillars of Islam) rather than being saved by grace through the redemptive sacrifice of Jesus Christ on the cross. We will never be able to share this Gospel (Good News) with Muslims in the most effective way unless we first recognize the cultural obstacles we put in their way and do our best to remove them.

In order to help you see these obstacles and to avoid pitfalls, I will provide some examples to start your thinking process. To do this, in the following chapters I will ask some questions and suggest answers. Have you ever stopped to consider why you are of the religion you belong to now? Have you ever considered changing your religion? If not, why not?

North America and Western Europe give freedom to Muslims to build mosques and worship in their own way—why aren't Muslim countries reciprocating? I know these are not one-size-fits-all situations. The answers given to these questions would vary in their application to different groups of Christians and different groups of Muslims. I will give a general overview; you will have to pick and choose what applies to your particular situation relative to Muslims.

Much of what is written in the Qur'an comes from the Old Testament or the Torah (the most holy of the sacred writings in Judaism). A lot of it is distorted and out of chronological order, but many of the teachings in the Qur'an are similar to Old Testament laws, such as the hope of salvation by works, not by grace. The Qur'an's way of relating to events is much more in line with the teaching of the Old Testament than with Christianity's New Testament doctrines, although some of the Qur'an's teachings do relate to the New Testament.

When speaking to a group in Colorado a few years ago, I mentioned that God also loved the now infamous Osama bin Laden and wanted to see him come to the knowledge of salvation. Afterward, a lady came to me and said she did not want to see Osama bin Laden in heaven. Wow! What an attitude. I was taken aback—I understood her feelings, but they are misguided.

We love the Apostle Paul of the New Testament. Our lives have been enriched by his letters to the churches and his teachings about Christian living. Sometimes we seem to forget that Paul used to be called Saul, and that prior to his conversion he had been doing all he could to persecute the followers of Jesus—he was the Osama bin Laden of his day. If Saul would have had access to explosives or airplanes, he might have done something similar to what Osama bin Laden did. He did his best with the means he had to persecute and destroy Jesus' followers. Until he knew better, he was convinced he was right.

Try to imagine the impact Osama bin Laden could have on the Muslim world if he had an experience similar to that of Saul on the road to Damascus. I think the reactions would be very similar to those after Saul's conversion—Christians would be afraid of him and Muslims would try to kill him before he could do too much damage to their cause. I do not say that, if caught, Osama bin Laden should not face charges for his crimes. Social justice would have to run its course.

We do live in a different world than in the days of Paul. I just like to reflect on the impact Osama bin Laden's conversion could have on the Muslim world. It could lead to millions of Muslims accepting *Isa Al-Masih* as their Lord and Savior. Wouldn't that be better than simply getting the "good news" that Osama bin Laden has finally been captured or killed? It is sad to say, but I think some Christians would prefer his capture or death to his salvation.

Romans 10:1–4 says:

Brothers, my heart's desire and prayer to God for the Israelites is that they may be saved. For I can testify about them that they are zealous for God, but their zeal is not based on knowledge. Since they did not know the righteousness that comes from God and sought to establish their own, they did not submit to God's righteousness. Christ is the end of the law so that there may be righteousness for everyone who believes.

The message in this passage applies to everyone. "Israelites" could easily be replaced with people of other religions, including Islam. If Paul would have lived in the Muslim world instead of the Jewish world, I believe he would have written "Brothers, my heart's desire and prayer for the *Muslims* is that they may be saved. For I can testify about the *Muslims* that they are zealous for God, but their zeal is not based on knowledge. Since the *Muslims* did not know the righteousness of God and sought to establish their own, they did not submit to God's righteousness." We have to admit that many Muslims are zealous for God, but their zeal, unfortunately, is not based on knowledge. They are trying to establish their own righteousness based on their ideas of good works.

It is important to notice that even though Paul knew that the Jews of his day were in the dark as far as God's plan of salvation is concerned, and that many of them were hypocrites and often violent and abusive, Paul still attended the synagogues. Whenever he went to a new place to teach about Jesus, he started by attending their synagogue and presenting the Gospel there. Perhaps we should try attending a mosque and, in that way, build relationships in order to have the opportunity to present the Gospel to our Muslim friends.

I have personally attended a mosque for prayers on numerous occasions and was very well received. It gave me excellent opportunities to share the Gospel. But that is another story, and it is not my intention to get into the contextualization debate right now. Much has been written by different authors on how much a person should or should not try to contextualize their outreach to Muslims. I would encourage anyone who is serious about sharing the Gospel with Muslims to search out and read some of the books and articles written by some of the authors involved in this debate. Three good possibilities to start with include *Muslim Evangelism: Contemporary Approaches to Contextualization*[1] by Phil Parshall, "Contextualization: Building Bridges to the Muslim Community"[2] by Jim Leffel, and "The C1 to C6 Spectrum: A Practical Tool for Defining Six Types of 'Christ-centered Communities' Found in the Muslim Context"[3] by John Travis.

Chapter Three

CHRISTIAN OR
MUSLIM—WHY?

HAVE YOU EVER STOPPED TO CONSIDER why you are a part of the religion you belong to now? Did you ever give serious thought to changing? Many people I have talked to have never really stopped and asked themselves these questions. They could give me all kinds of good reasons why they believe the way they do, but none had really considered the cultural background that usually contributes to the basis of their faith.

My father and mother were born in Quebec. The province of Quebec, being French-speaking and tracing its roots to France, was 95 percent Catholic. The rest of Canada, being mostly of English descent, was and still is largely Protestant. I come from a large family. My parents had twelve children, which was perfectly normal when I was a teenager. Most of our neighbors had ten or more children. It was part of our French, Catholic culture.

My parents had a small farm and having many offspring meant more help in its operation. Things have changed, however, and now if anyone would have a family of twelve or more in Quebec, people would be most surprised. That family might well become a tourist attraction. Can you imagine what it would mean today to have twelve children?

First of all, you would need a school bus to go places with all the laws about car seats for children and seat belts. However, you might be able to get group rates at restaurants and on airlines. Fortunately, with that many kids in one family, not all are small at the same time. By the time the last one is born, the older children are likely to have moved out of the house, be married, and have kids of their own. Neither I, nor any of my siblings, have more than three children. Modernization has influenced and changed our culture.

Before I was born, my mother, on her own initiative, had left Catholicism and become a Protestant. She had not chosen to be born a Catholic, but being born into a Catholic family made her a Catholic. At that time, my father did go to church, but was not serious about his religion. Many French Canadians still call themselves Catholics, but most are only nominally so.

I grew up a Protestant because by then that is what my family had become. Three of my older siblings had gone to Bible school. Our mother had taken us to Sunday school since the time we were small and we automatically belonged to the Protestant church. We lived in the north of Quebec and many of our friends were Cree Indians. Just as they had no say in being born Cree, I had no say in being born a White French Canadian, nor in being born a Protestant. It was not until I was a teenager that I started to wonder why I was a Protestant.

I began to question my faith—how could I be so sure that being a Protestant was the right thing? Most of our relatives were Catholics, and they were convinced that Catholicism was the best religion. I had also heard of devotees to other faiths such as the Mormons, the Jehovah's Witnesses, Muslims, and Hindus. I assumed that all of them were sure their faith was the best. Why would they think differently? After all, in most cases, the entire family would be of the same persuasion, as well as their friends and many of the people with whom they went to school or worked. So why should they even question whether or not they have the right faith? Why risk being alienated from all their family and friends if they are happy where they are?

The religion you belong to is very much like the language group of which you are a part. Had I been born in China, I would most likely speak Mandarin or Cantonese, depending on where in China I had been born, and it is equally likely that I would be a Buddhist or an atheist. Had I been born in Pakistan, I would probably speak Urdu and be a Muslim.

Most people belong to their religion not by choice, but by birth and family tradition—just as a person who grew up speaking French or English or German or Swahili did so not by choice, but by birth. Those born into a minority language group often grow up also speaking—or later learn—the dominant language of their surroundings. Similarly, people born into a minority religion may eventually adopt, in part or completely, the majority religion practiced in their area. In both cases it might be done for nothing more than convenience.

In developing countries, people often need to learn the national language to attend school, especially for higher education. There they will likely be surrounded by people of the majority religion; to fit in, many accept the majority faith. As seen all over Africa, students from animist families attending Catholic schools will often declare themselves Catholics, whether they are true practitioners or not.

Then there are people who simply choose to learn a new language for the pleasure of learning it or for material advantage. In the same way there are those who explore a new religion out of curiosity, for material advantage, because of lack of fulfillment in their own religion, or because of the invitation of a friend. People from minority language groups suffer from a shortage of written material in their mother tongue—people of minority religions have a similar problem. In addition, if they travel outside their immediate area, they might not find anyone who practices religion the way in which they are accustomed.

What happens when you leave the area where your mother tongue is used and you have to learn a new language? You meet new people and often develop a new circle of friends. If you want to become fluent, you may have to move to a different area or country. This can be very difficult and emotionally demanding. The new language is difficult at first—cultural expressions and the entire cultural baggage that come with the mother tongue may have to be abandoned and a new way of life learned. So much of our culture is reflected in our original language—the expressions we use and even the structure of our sentences. That is why you can often recognize where a person is from by the way he speaks or forms phrases. For many people, a change in language setting is more than they can handle; because of this, they choose not to learn a foreign language even if they see definite advantages in speaking it. Some will reach a certain threshold in language acquisition but never progress very far for the same reasons.

Just as it can be very difficult to learn a new language and adapt to it, some of the challenges of adopting a new religion can be intimidating to the point of being prohibitive. Changes will occur that are similar to linguistic study. Frequently it will mean distancing oneself from one's family. Often a new way of life has to be learned. What a person previously considered important will suddenly be irrelevant.

The change can be especially difficult when it comes to special religious holidays during which the family traditionally gets together to celebrate. For people raised in Christian traditions, it might mean giving up the custom of getting together with the family at Christmas; for those with small children it might mean no Easter eggs or Easter Bunny—even no Thanksgiving dinner.

For Muslims it may mean no fasting for the month of Ramadan and not being part of all the festivities that last for a whole week at the end of the fasting month. For the animist it may mean rejection by the family for refusing to take part in an animal sacrifice that is supposed to bring protection against evil spirits or ensure good crops and then being blamed by the family or the entire village if the rains do not come and the crops fail.

Understandably, for most people, it is heart-wrenching to walk away from their family and community and along with it all the attendant relationships and activities that also have a bearing on marriage, inheritance, or business partnerships. The whole complex web of inter-relationships holds a person to the religion of his family and community.

Many who would want to join a new religious group for whatever reason will not do so for fear of reprisals, the loss of friendships, fear of the unknown, or loss of position in their community. They see the price to be paid for changing as higher than they are willing or able to pay. Many, not having counted the cost, will abandon the effort. Jesus said, "The one who received the seed that fell on rocky places is the man who hears the word and at once receives it with joy. But since he has no root, he lasts only a short time. When trouble or persecution comes because of the word, he quickly falls away. The one who received the seed that fell among the thorns is the man who hears the word, but the worries of this life and the deceitfulness of wealth choke it, making it unfruitful" (Matthew 13:20–22).

It is important to be sensitive to what is simply cultural and what is actually required by God's Word. By carefully distinguishing between the two, it is possible to diminish the negative social cost of changing religions. It is a matter of not causing unnecessary disruptions and placing heavy burdens on the person endeavoring to change. "Therefore let us stop passing judgment on one another. Instead, make up your mind not to put any stumbling block or obstacle in your brother's way." (See Romans 14:5–13.)

Many people who are born within a large language group, such as English, French, or German, may never see or feel the need to learn a new language because they are perfectly satisfied with their language, friends, and position in society. In the same way, those born into major religious groups may never see or feel a need to change. Why should they? Their religion is part of their culture and often encompasses most aspects of their lives, such as family relations, marriages, funerals, and work relationships.

Most people do not change their religion or faith without strong reasons. I have known cases where people went through major upheaval simply by changing from one group of Protestants to another. A lady once told me that after she changed from being a member of a Church of Christ church to being a member of a Friends church, her grandfather considered her lost and prayed daily for her to repent and be saved. However, going from one Protestant church to another Protestant church or even from a Protestant church to a Catholic church is not at all as drastic as leaving Islam to become a Christian. It can be much more costly and dramatic for the people involved, often involving death threats.

Chapter Four

HAVE YOU EVER SERIOUSLY CONSIDERED CHANGING RELIGION?

If Not, Why Not?

A COUPLE OF YEARS AGO, a friend of mine was working among Muslims and enjoyed debating with them, comparing the Bible with the Qur'an. He had been a cheerful young man, but for some time I had been noticing that something seemed to be bothering him. Whenever I asked him how things were going, he would simply say that all was fine.

In a restaurant one day, I asked him again. This time his answer was straightforward: "I am thinking about becoming a Muslim." Knowing that he had been a committed Christian and a Bible college graduate, I did not take him seriously. I thought he was joking and that he had some serious problem that he did not want to talk about—that his answer was simply a way to avoid talking about what was really bothering him.

One day not long after that—to my surprise and to that of most of his friends—he went to a mosque and made a public declaration that he was renouncing his Christian faith and becoming a Muslim. He recited the *Shahada* saying, "There is no God but Allah, and Mohammed is his prophet." Reciting the *Shahada* is a formal part of becoming a Muslim, rather like the ceremony of baptism for a Christian.

At first he was zealous in his new faith, trying to convert other Christians. But after a few months he secretly made contact with some of his old Christian friends, seeking help in getting away from Islam because he feared for his life. He admitted to having been lured by promises of financial help and celebrity made by his Muslim contacts. But these were not forthcoming and once he was not pampered anymore as a new convert, he realized that his new faith did not give him the satisfaction he thought he would have. He has now moved to another country and is trying to rebuild his life, having lost the trust and respect of his friends from both groups.

In recent years, there have been many conversions to Islam among African-Americans. Probably few of the converts had been committed Christians. Many conversions have taken place in prison among African-American inmates. To them, Islam has become the religious equivalent of a political party or a special-interest club. Plus, it gives them a sense of belonging to a large family, similar to African tribal membership. They have been told to return to their roots, to the religion of their ancestors.

However, that is misleading since most Black Africans were animists, not Muslims. They have been asked why they would follow the religion of the same people who had held them as slaves and often still treat them as second-class citizens. The truth is that in Africa today, Muslim Moors and Sudanese Arabs still have Black African slaves and Arabs generally regard Black Africans as inferior, even primitive.

The answer to my opening question in this chapter is probably "No." It is not likely that you have ever seriously considered changing religion. The idea probably did not even occur to you. Why would you want to anyway? Life is complicated enough as it is. You have enough problems already; why ask for more? You probably took the religion of your parents, whether or not they actually practiced it. If you already have a religion, why would you even think of becoming a Muslim, for example? Besides, there are plenty of reasons why you would not want to follow Islam.

What comes to your mind when you think about Islam? Since 9–11, hardly a day goes by when you don't hear or read something negative about it. The example is often cited of the way the women were abused in Afghanistan under the Taliban regime and continue to be abused in some other Muslim countries. You see photos of women in the hottest climates on the planet covered head to toe in voluminous black garments. For some of us, this is considered discrimination and oppression, although others would debate that view.

You hear about suicide bombers blowing themselves up in markets all over Iraq and other places. They are no longer primarily targeting military installations, but civilians, since they are soft targets. They are not only fighting against the "foreign devils," but much of the time also among themselves. They seem to have no respect for human life. It makes me cringe when I listen to the news and hear of more suicide bombers killing the innocent.

Since 9–11 we all have had to put up with previously unknown restrictions because of Muslim extremists plotting more terrorist attacks against your country. Just think of boarding an airplane. You can no longer even carry a nail file on board with you. You often have to remove your shoes, coat and belt, have your hand luggage searched, and occasionally submit to body searches when going through security. Life has become much more complicated because of the declared goal of militant Muslims to rule the world. Security concerns add a huge financial burden to the economy. It can seem like the word "Muslim" spells trouble.

In my opinion, most North Americans and Western Europeans who convert to Islam do not do it out of the conviction that Islam is superior to Christianity or that being a Muslim will get them into heaven when they die. Instead they do it to express their resentment toward a failed and failing society. It gives them an outlet to vent their animosity and hatred toward democracy and to rail against the discrimination, poverty, low moral standards, and injustice they see in the western world.

Obviously, they have reasons to be frustrated with the way justice is administered at times, but aside from the comfort they may get by joining a group that is anti-anything North American or western in nature, they soon realize that things are not all rosy in Islam either. There is plenty of corruption, and injustice abounds in Muslim countries also. Indonesia, which has the world's largest Muslim population, rates among the most corrupt countries on the globe. Even in Muslim countries that claim to have freedom of religion, devotees of minority religions are persecuted and harassed by intolerant Muslims while their governments turn a blind eye.

All of these reasons should be more than enough to turn away any intelligent seeker who might have considered converting to Islam. It seems obvious to us that any Muslim who would seriously consider the matter would question his faith and realize that Christianity and its value system is superior to his own. We think he should not have to deliberate much about that; he should do all he can to know more about Christianity so he can have the opportunity to become a Christian. Is that not what many Christians think?

Now, let's take the time to consider the other side of the coin. We have talked about the things that turn most of us away from Islam. Other than its appeal to primarily African-American prison inmates through its ability to create a sense of belonging, we have found little in Islam that would attract us. Let us put ourselves into the shoes of a Muslim, and let us juxtapose the factors that would be attractive to us in Christianity to the factors that may turn us away from Christianity.

To Christians, believing in salvation by grace through the sacrifice of Jesus on the cross not only is a historical fact, it is also superior to a remote hope of earning salvation through our own works and/or by the observance of the Five Pillars of Islam. Many Muslims feel—and rightly so—that Christians abuse the concept of grace and use it as an excuse to indulge in sinful activities. In doing so, Christians erroneously believe that on the Day of Judgment, God, being merciful, will wipe away their willful sins.

When it was pointed out to an eloquent Imam that Muslims do not believe in the grace of God, he explained how Muslims view salvation by grace through this example: It is like a university student who puts in neither the effort in class nor the hours in study to adequately prepare for his exams, being overly confident that he can wing it. That student might be in for a rude awakening. He might find out that he was not as ready as he thought. He may find out, albeit too late, that he flunked his classes.

The Imam went on to say that Christians do the same with grace. They think that there is no problem—that they can wing it and grace will see them through "the Pearly Gates." They may well realize too late, however, that they did not quite make it—that if, perhaps, they had been more serious about their faith, the end result would have been better. Now, who would argue with that?

Christians rightly have good reasons to believe that the Bible is the inspired Word of God, that it has God's plan of salvation for humankind, that Jesus died on the cross and paid the price for them when they did not deserve it, and that it is by his grace (not by their works) that they are saved. No human being can attain to the righteousness of God on his own and deserve, through his own doing, forgiveness for his sins. One would think this should be enough to convince anyone that Christianity is superior to Islam. What is it then that keeps Muslims from understanding this and yielding their lives to Jesus?

It may appear that I am acting as the devil's advocate, but don't you think that to those who grew up in other religions, the Christian claim to having the only way to salvation and eternal life in heaven would sound presumptuous? When Christians tell Muslims that theirs is the only way, they are essentially saying that all Muslims are wrong and on their way to a lost eternity. Not an easy pill to swallow. Not the type of thing you want to hear before going to bed, let alone your death bed. Jesus says in John 14:6, "I am the way and the truth and the life. No one comes to the Father except through me."

Still, in the desire to reach the lost, a person must look perceptively through the eyes of those he seeks to reach for Christ. It is important to understand that Muslims also believe that theirs is the only way to salvation and that *you* are the one who is on the way to hell.

John 3:1–21 gives a perfect example of how we can share the Good News. When Jesus was approached by Nicodemus at night, he did not immediately confront him, telling him he was on his way to hell and that he had better shape up and do something about it here and now. Instead Jesus used words like "you need to be born again," "for God so loved the world," "whoever believes in him is not condemned"—words that are uplifting, positive and encouraging instead of threatening and condemning. The reality of eternity without Christ has to be made real, but emphasis should be put on the grace of God and the gift of salvation instead of on the coming Judgment Day.

We have just been talking about all the things that make Islam repulsive to you, about all the things you hear and read that make you cringe. What information about Christianity do you think Muslims read in newspapers, hear on the radio, or see on television in their countries? Do the newspaper headlines herald all the good things genuine Christians do? Even in our own country, the press is by and large unfavorable toward Christians and at times even downright scornful. Remember that in most Muslims countries freedom of the press (as we know it) does not exist. Freedom of the press to them means freedom to praise your political and religious leaders. It does not mean freedom to criticize them, irrespective of what they have been doing.

The things that make media headlines in Muslim countries (although not exclusively there) include events such as the school massacres at Columbine High School in Colorado and at Virginia Tech; problems of drug addiction, pornography, and gambling; disunity in churches and splits over issues like abortion and homosexuality; debates over the ordination of gay priests and bishops as well as same-sex marriage (it is bad enough that those topics are discussed among unbelievers, they should certainly not be an issue in the church); and a church-going United States president having sex with his aide in the Oval Office and denying it under oath.

These are not at all things that bring honor to Christianity and to the Lord Jesus, but like it or not, you are part of these problems and debates. If you were not already a Christian, would you seriously consider joining a religion with a reputation associated with these types of problems? Probably not.

You may protest, "No, I am not like that. My church does not have those problems. We know right from wrong." Face it: Your good name as a Christian has been tarnished by the actions of others. You are guilty by association. As far as Muslims are concerned, Christians are Christians, just as in your eyes, Muslims are Muslims. They do not distinguish between cultural Christians, namely those who are categorized as Christians because they happen to be born in the West, and those who are true believers.

If you are Caucasian, chances are you are identified by many non-westerners as Christian, even though only a small minority of westerners are genuine followers of Jesus. Just as you defend yourself and the reputation of your faith, most Muslims would correctly tell you they are not all terrorists, that they do not all believe in violence and suicide bombings. They would also say that those who do such things are a very small minority of misguided fanatics. Unfortunately, their number is growing, and it is no longer such a small minority.

I asserted earlier that it seems at times Muslims have no respect for human life when suicide bombers engage in indiscriminate killings. What do you think comes to the minds of Muslims when they read and hear about the more than one million babies that are killed each year in abortion clinics in the western world, in those "Christian" nations? Would they think that Christians have respect for human life?

Yes, some abortions do take place in Muslim countries, but they are not approved by either the state or by Islam. Abortions are illegal and considered wrong and immoral. The Qur'an 6:140 and 152 has this to say: "Losers indeed are they who kill their children foolishly out of ignorance and make unlawful that which Allah has provided for them, fabricating a lie against Allah" and, "Say, O Prophet: Come, let me rehearse to you that which our Lord has enjoined: that you associate not anything as partner with him; that you behave benevolently towards your parents; that you destroy not your offspring for fear of poverty, it is we who provide for you and for them; that you approach not evil of any kind whether manifest or hidden; that you destroy not the life that Allah has declared sacred, except for just cause."

Mohammed may have been talking about infanticide, but it applies equally to abortion. Chapter 17:32 says, "Do not destroy your offspring for fear of poverty; it is we who provide for them and for you. Surely, destroying them is a great sin." The Qur'an is obviously unambiguous when it comes to forbidding taking the life of your child. The more than 40 million babies who have been aborted since *Roe vs. Wade* have contributed further to America's degraded reputation in the Islamic world. While Islamic extremists kill for political or religious reasons, westerners kill for convenience.

In this chapter I did not paint a very positive picture of Islam, and I painted an equally grim picture of so-called Christianity. I have often heard people who work among Muslims state that Christians themselves are the biggest obstacle to Muslims becoming believers in Jesus Christ. Christians are supposed to reflect the glory of Christ, but I am afraid that what is reflected is often not at all glorious. It is, in fact, often rather appalling!

Chapter Five

WHY AREN'T MODERATE MUSLIMS DOING MORE TO STOP EXTREMISTS IN THEIR MIDST?

"WHY DON'T YOU DO SOMETHING ABOUT THIS?" Has anyone ever asked you that in a reproachful tone? Wanting to do something about a situation and actually being able to achieve a change are two different things.

On the afternoon of September 11, 2001, I was in a small village in Mali, West Africa, and walked into a shop to greet my Fulani friend whose dad owned the place. In the United States, the tragic events of 9–11 had happened just a few hours earlier, and being in a remote village, I was still blissfully unaware of what had taken place. A television behind his shop counter was showing pictures, transmitted from France, of two airplanes crashing into the two World Trade Center towers in New York City and of the Pentagon in flames.

My first thought was, *The world will never be the same.* I was right; the world, indeed, is not and never will be the same. My friend Abdoulaye and a few other customers there did not seem unduly disturbed by what they were seeing. They were all Muslims, but like most Malians, not of the militant sort. Their comments were mostly that the United States "had it coming" and for them, business would go on as usual—or so they thought.

Fearing more attacks, we have seen all kinds of security measures set in place. There has been more violence: the bombings of the train in Madrid, the bombings of the subway in London, an explosive-laden Jeep crashed into an airport in Scotland, and numerous other terrorist atrocities. Other plots, fortunately, have been foiled.

Many countries are involved in the "war on terror," a conflict considered by many Muslims to be a war on Islam (not that some Muslims didn't bring it upon themselves by their actions). More and more the "war on terror" is framed in terms of "us against them," the West against the Arabs and the rest of the Muslim world. This struggle is like a grass fire. You try to stomp it out in one place, but it springs up in several others a few feet away. Attempts at putting down a terrorist cell in one place are followed by three others popping up elsewhere.

From the very beginning, the conduct of this war on terror has spurred violent debates in the halls of power around the world. Everyone is pointing fingers at others for errors that have been made; everyone thinks their methods would have worked better. By now, all these know-it-alls should also recognize that there is no easy way to fight terrorism, no easy way to fight religious ideologies that are inflamed by hatred, ignorance, and political agendas. In countries where Muslims make up a large majority, Islam tends to permeate every aspect of life and politics.

Western nations are different from the Islamic world. We have totally different cultures and forms of government—ours is secular, theirs is profoundly influenced by religious aspirations. It is democracy versus theocracy and/or autocracy, and each is unable to see the world or God through the other's cultural eyes. Each assumes that others should have the same viewpoint and priorities as he does and interpret God's will as he sees it. Consequently, each group is unable to understand the other and why they act and react as they do.

Why, then, are moderate Muslims not doing more to stop Islamic extremists? With all its military might, the West has not been able to stop Muslim terrorism. Instead, it seems to have done more to stir up the fire. How then do you think the governments of Muslim countries, assuming they do want to stomp it out in their own countries, can stop extremism?

Some leaders and influential people in the Islamic world have spoken out against violence and promoted tolerance and dialogue. Among them are His Highness the Aga Khan, spiritual leader of Shia Ismaili Muslims; Her Majesty Queen Rania Al Abdullah of the Hashemite Kingdom of Jordan; and Abdurrahman Wahid, ex-president of Indonesia. Think about the conflict between Protestants and Catholics in Northern Ireland that has lasted over thirty years. A forest fire is certainly easier to ignite than to put out.

Not long ago someone asked me that initial question: "Why aren't moderate Muslims doing more to stop extremists in their midst?" I responded with a question of my own: "I assume you are against abortion. Tell me, what have you personally done to stop abortion in this country?"

He stood there looking at me with his mouth half open. Bull's eye! He didn't know what to say. I do not know whether or not he had ever tried to fight abortion, but obviously he had not been successful. Many people who dislike abortion aren't committed enough to their convictions to join anti-abortion rallies, peacefully picket in front of abortion clinics, or volunteer at crisis pregnancy centers. After all, don't people have to be careful not to be seen as politically incorrect or bigots? People may rail against abortion with their families or friends, but getting out of their comfort zone and actually doing something is another story.

Fortunately, some Christians, churches, and organizations have taken a stand against abortion and have done excellent work in exposing its widespread practice and have fought it at political and judicial levels. They are fighting the good fight as Paul says in 1 Timothy 6:12: "Fight the good fight of the faith." Nevertheless, we are told that still over one million babies are killed by abortion each year in the U.S. alone.

It is not that Christians have not tried. Jesus' words in Luke 22:53b hit the nail on the head: "But this is your hour—when darkness reigns." Darkness reigns in this world. Satan is doing all he can to create confusion and chaos, to turn people against each other, to sow hatred in every heart that is not filled with the love of God. Christians who are not careful can easily succumb to that hatred—hating Muslims for what some of them have done and continue to do. Sectarian hatred keeps the cycle of violence going.

If well-intentioned Christians, churches, and religious organizations have not been able to do more to stop the scourge of abortion, what do you think impoverished and often poorly educated Muslims can do to stop Islamic terrorists in their own country, let alone in other parts of the world?

A few of the people in positions of influence such as imams, professors in Islamic universities and journalists in the Muslim media have ventured to speak out against the extremists.

Some of the few who have dared to take a public stand against terrorism have been threatened or killed. Many Iraqis tried to support the coalition troops and ended up paying with their lives. If we Christians in the West, with all our freedom of expression, are too cowardly or too complacent to take a bold stand against abortion and other moral problems for fear of being mocked or seen as intolerant, how do you think Muslims, who could risk their lives or those of their loved ones, feel about speaking up against extremist elements in their midst?

I used to criticize Jonah for disobeying God when he was told to go to Nineveh and call the people to repentance lest they perish in forty days. After all, God had asked him personally to go preach so they might turn from their evil ways. What an honor to be asked by God Almighty to go preach his Word. How would you respond if God, in a clear, audible voice, told you, "My friend, I want you to go to Tehran. Walk up and down the streets for forty days and tell them, 'Repent or perish!'"? Tarshish would suddenly look like a nice place to go. Perhaps God, realizing you are busy, would ask someone else.

Pray that God will give you the courage to speak against all evil—not only that of the Islamic extremists, but also against that of abortionists and the general decadence of the western world. Ask him to give you a love for your fellowmen, including those who happen to be Muslim. Pray that he will help you see through their cultural eyes and understand their repulsion for the depravity they see associated with Christianity.

Chapter Six

TALK ABOUT BEING UNFAIR!

NORTH AMERICA AND WESTERN EUROPE give freedom to Muslims to build mosques and worship in their own way. Why aren't Muslim countries reciprocating?

The more the world becomes the global village that politicians argue about, the more it is a given that inter-country relationships must be based on reciprocity. Whether the issue is commerce, monetary policy—even student exchange—to have peaceful coexistence, understanding and good will, it is imperative that international cooperation be mutually beneficial.

There are now more than two thousand mosques in the U.S. In England thirty years ago there were only three. Today, they number more than five thousand! The largest mosque in the world is now in the heart of London. (See *Islam in the Balance*.[1]) While in some places churches are closing for lack of interest and are being demolished or turned into museums, mosques are coming up everywhere like dandelions in springtime.

While Islam is aggressively expanding in the West, in some Muslim countries opponents of Christianity are burning down existing church buildings and forcing others to close using all kinds of trumped-up charges. Indonesia, which is supposed to have freedom of religion, has a law that requires that Christians, in order to start a new church, must first obtain signatures from at least sixty neighbors declaring that they have no objection to a new church in their neighborhood. What are the chances of that happening in a predominantly Muslim country? At the same time, new mosques and *mushallahs* (rooms for collective prayer) dot the neighborhoods, with new ones opening regularly without proper permits.

I have often pointed out to Muslim friends the injustice of it all. While they immigrate to North America and Europe and claim their assumed "rights," most of them wouldn't dream of giving the same rights to adherents of minority religions in their own countries. They want, as it were, to have *their* cake and eat *yours*, too. Our gullibility must have them laughing. It is getting so bad that it is no longer a joking matter. Their demands not only have spiritual implications, but political ones as well.

Muslim organizers in the West have been granted permission to build mosques, and in some places have agitated for and received the right to broadcast the call to prayer five times a day via loudspeakers set high on their minarets. In Islamic countries they start the call to prayer as early as 4:30 in the morning. Have you ever stayed in a house across the street from a mosque in a Muslim country?

Many Islamic communities now want Muslim holidays to be added to North American calendars and all public schools closed for their holidays, essentially demanding rights equal to the Christian traditions, even though they are a small minority. In North America, schools and offices do not close for Jewish, Hindu, or Buddhist holidays. Not in your wildest dreams would anyone dare suggest similar rights for Christians in Saudi Arabia, the home of Mecca, Islam's holiest city and place of pilgrimage. Most other Muslim countries would be no more welcoming. Is that fair? No, of course not! So why are Muslims, who are supposed to be peace-loving and tolerant of other religions, behaving that way?

Muslims are supposed to be tolerant of Christians and Jews as long as they are willing to submit to Islamic rule. In the Qur'an, 9:29 it says, "Fight those among the people of the Book who believe not in Allah, nor in the last day, nor hold as unlawful that which Allah and his messenger have declared to be unlawful nor follow the true religion, and who have not yet made peace with you, until they pay the tax willingly and make their submission." (The Qur'an refers to both Jews and Christians as "people of the Book.") Over the centuries, Muslim scholars have interpreted this passage in various ways. Based on that passage, some countries have implemented laws that are very restrictive to Christians, while others have been less strict. Saudi Arabia, which finances the building of mosques worldwide with its oil revenues, strictly forbids church building in its own country, while some less intransigent Islamic states allow it.

Nevertheless, in most areas, Muslims are uncompromising toward non-Muslims. They do not intend to grant the rights they demand from their host countries in the West to minorities in their own countries. One day, when they become the majority in a host country, they will do all in their power to impose their Islamic laws and regulations on non-Muslims. It is what their religion demands.

As stated earlier, much of the Qur'an consists of fragments extracted from the Old Testament. As the Israelites prepared to take the Promised Land, what did God command them to do in Deuteronomy 7:1–6?

> When the LORD your God brings you into the land you are enter-ing to possess and drives out before you many nations—the Hittites, Girgashites, Amorites, Canaanites, Perizzites, Hivites and Jebusites, seven nations larger and stronger than you—and when the LORD your God has delivered them over to you and you have defeated them, then you must destroy them totally. Make no treaty with them, and show them no mercy. Do not intermarry with them. Do not give your daughters to their sons or take their daughters for your sons, for they will turn your sons away from following me to serve other gods, and the LORD's anger will burn against you and will quickly destroy you. This is what you are to do with them: Break down their altars, smash their sacred stones, cut down their Asherah poles and burn their idols in the fire. For you are a people holy to the LORD your God. The LORD your God has chosen you out of all the peoples on the face of the earth to be his people, his treasured possession.

Of course, you may rightly claim that we are not one of those seven nations recorded here. After all this was said to the Israelites, not to Muslims—and certainly not to or about North America and Western

Europe. True, but what I am trying to point out is that if a religion is based on parts of the Old Testament and its adherents try to transpose its teaching intended for another time period into today's world, you get fanatics who are totally intolerant of other religions and are bound by what they see as God's will: to fight and destroy the "infidels." Most Muslims see the West as immoral and ungodly. As Christians, can we deny that? We know that not all westerners are immoral and ungodly, but we can't deny either that a great many of them are.

Many Muslims wonder why Christians can be so tolerant of the immorality that surrounds them and ask why we don't do more to stop it. They can see that just as God warned in Deuteronomy that by being overly tolerant and indifferent, many Christians have become worldly and immoral themselves. Their hearts have been turned away from God to a secular culture that pushes ever further the envelope of acceptability. Muslim extremists think they have a God-given mandate to fight on his behalf and kill and destroy in any possible way all the infidels. Yet, many of those extremists are themselves corrupt and immoral.

Considering the goal of some Islamists to establish the rule of a Caliphate (an empire controlled by a secular and spiritual successor of Mohammed) over the entire world, it is as much a political war as a religious one. History repeats itself. Intrepid explorers and pioneers paved the way for their respective European countries that then fought, conquered, and colonized large areas to expand their power base. In the process, they introduced Christianity. Explorers who ventured to North and South America from Europe were not only commissioned by their rulers, but by the Catholic Church, as well. In some cases, Christian missionaries were given wide freedoms and political authority, which was sometimes misused. Muslims, encouraged by the unofficial sixth pillar of Islam, jihad, are doing all they can to expand their political and religious power.

Are Muslims right? Have Christians become too tolerant of the immorality that abounds around them? It seems that unbelievers have a greater influence over believers than vice versa. Christians in many cases are not the salt and light of the earth as they should be. They have become insipid and are being sucked into the ways of the world. Christians should not imitate Muslims and take up arms against their neighbors whom they consider unrighteous, but certainly should do more to keep themselves from being polluted by the world around them. "Religion that God our Father accepts as pure and faultless is this: to look after orphans and widows in their distress and to keep oneself from being polluted by the world" (James 1:27).

Most of us have heard of the dire punishments that can await a Muslim who leaves Islam. He or she can suffer all kinds of physical and mental torture and even be put to death by his or her friends, family members, or an Islamic court. Here is a good example of the situation in Pakistan from an article in *WORLD Magazine*[2]:

> Most ominous for Christian believers, who are not named in this story due to the present dangers they face, is a measure pushed before parliament May 9 creating stiffer penalties for anyone who leaves Islam. Under the new Apostasy Act, a male accused of departing Islam will receive the death penalty. Women apostates will be imprisoned for life, or until they "repent." Those found guilty forfeit all property rights and lose legal custody of their children.

In marked contrast, when a Christian abandons his or her faith, the consequences from family and friends are generally minor. Again, this will vary from family to family, from one Christian group to another, but, on the whole, even if their decision is deplored, no physical persecution or torture will ensue.

What did the Old Testament law have to say about similar cases?

> If your very own brother, or your own son or daughter, or the wife you love, or your closest friend secretly entices you, saying, "Let us go and worship other gods" (gods that neither you nor your fathers have known, gods of the people around you, whether near or far, from one end of the land to the other), do not yield to him or listen to him. Show him no pity. Do not spare him or shield

him. You must certainly put him to death. Your hand must be the first in putting him to death, and then the hands of all the people. Stone him to death, because he tried to turn you away from the LORD your God, who brought you out of Egypt, out of the land of slavery. Then all Israel will hear and be afraid, and no one among you will do such an evil thing again. If you hear it said about one of the towns the LORD your God is giving you to live in that wicked men have arisen among you and have led the people of their town astray, saying, "Let us go and worship other gods" (gods you have not known), then you must inquire, probe and investigate it thoroughly. And if it is true and it has been proved that this detestable thing has been done among you, you must certainly put to the sword all who live in that town. Destroy it completely, both its people and its livestock (Deuteronomy 13:6–15).

That was drastic. Muslims, who try to follow customs similar to this Old Testament one, are convinced that religious regulations should still be enforced to the same extent today. How can they understand the New Testament principle of grace and freedom if they have not had the chance to have it explained to them? As Paul says in Romans 10:14: "How, then, can they call on the one they have not believed in? And how can they believe in the one of whom they have not heard? And how can they hear without someone preaching to them?" They can't understand why Christians, genuine or not, do not act as they themselves do toward infidels—and this leads them to believe that Christians are not serious about their faith.

More and more Muslim countries now refuse visas to Christians who wish to enter as missionaries. Christians feel this is unfair on their part. Why should they keep missionaries out? Are they afraid Christians have something better to offer than what they already have? It is reminiscent of the restrictions under the old Soviet Union. Muslims are not denied entry into America on the basis of their religion (although they certainly are screened more carefully now), so why should Christian missionaries be restricted entry into their countries?

How would you feel if you knew that the Arab family who just moved in next door (with the man who wears a dress) was here as Muslim missionaries? Their goal and full-time occupation are to convert Christians to Islam. How would you feel about having your kids play with their kids or having your teenagers hang around their house? Would you want to socialize with them? A normal reaction would be caution. "I want you to stay away from those people. They are here to convert you, change your faith, and make you believe a bunch of lies. They might even try to turn you against us and recruit you to become terrorists." That would be a perfectly normal reaction, and who could blame you? Why, then, should Muslims feel differently about Christian missionaries coming to convert them and their children?

Muslims love their children, too, and family ties among them are often stronger than they are among families in the West. Moreover, their standing as a family in the community is very important to them, as is an individual's standing in his family and a nuclear family's among their relatives. When a person leaves the faith, it is a major embarrassment to the whole family and damages their standing in the community. A convert to Christ brings shame to his whole extended family and even to the entire community. Seen in that light, it is easier to understand why Muslims want to take all measures possible to prevent apostasy from happening to one of their own.

Would it not be terribly embarrassing if your son were to become a devotee of the Hare Krishna movement, walking down the streets with his head shaved except for a tiny pony tail, wearing an orange robe, and distributing leaflets? In India, that may be all right, but in your culture such behavior is not normal.

Among Muslim families, leaving Islam is even more despised as it puts the family in a very difficult position with the community. They may be pushed by the rest of the community to severely punish that person—even kill the apostate—if he or she will not recant. Even though parents would prefer not to hurt their child, they also know that God and the community should come first. Comparing the severity of Islamic sentiments towards those who leave the faith with the natural family and community bonds, it is easy to imagine the dilemma facing the relatives of converts to Christ.

Does that mean that in order to avoid putting the families in such a position, no one should share the Good News with them? Has the "Good News" become "bad news" to them? No, but the sharing has to be done in love and with an understanding of the cultural ramifications. "But thanks be to God, who always leads us in triumphal procession in Christ and through us spreads everywhere the fragrance of the knowledge of him. For we are to God the aroma of Christ among those who are being saved and those who are perishing. To the one we are the smell of death; to the other, the fragrance of life. And who is equal to such a task?" (2 Corinthians 2:14–16).

Every effort should be made to keep the family together instead of pulling the new believer away from his family. Keep in mind that in a Muslim country the whole situation can become very stressful and even dangerous for the person who is sharing his faith with his Muslim friend as well as for the Muslim who is showing interest in Christ.

Chapter Seven

BUILDING BRIDGES

HOW THEN CAN WE BUILD BRIDGES between the followers of Christ and the followers of Islam? Can it be done without Christians having to compromise what they believe? Are Christians the ones who always have to "give in"? Can we trade "eyeglasses" and see through each other's cultural eyes?

For western countries to always bend over backwards to accommodate the demands of Muslims is not the right way to go about things. That is comparable to parents always giving in to the demands of a spoiled child in order to appease him. Demeaning as this may sound, I can think of no better illustration to demonstrate such a one-sided arrangement. Some parents are afraid to refuse any demands of their child, knowing that if he does not get what he wants, he will throw a fit. That child will always want more and will never be satisfied until he gets all he wants and rules the nest. The parents become hostages of their pampered child because they give in to his demands. Neither the parents nor the child are really winners in such a situation and it certainly does not make for happy living.

There has been a similar pattern of behavior among Muslims in their dealings with other countries and especially among Muslim immigrants in dealing with their host countries. Their attitude has often been, "You give me what I want and you give it to me now or else I will throw a fit. I will riot or put a bomb somewhere and kill a bunch of innocent people. I will do so until I get what I want."

We have seen how western governments cowered in front of Muslims after a Danish newspaper published cartoons of Mohammed that some

Muslims found offensive, and after the Pope made remarks about Muslim violence while on a visit to Germany in 2006. Our leaders have gone out of their way in an effort to show that they believe Muslims are peace-loving people (whether they actually believe this or not is another question), that we want to respect their rights, that we—not they—are the ones in the wrong, etc.

It is not right to purposely do things to anger Muslims and provoke them, just like it would not be right to purposely anger a child, but Muslims worldwide also have to learn to respect the rights of others. It would be improper for me to go to your house and tell you how you should behave in your home or dictate what you can or cannot say.

In the same way, Muslims should not assume they can impose their religion, customs, laws, or way of thinking on the rest of the world, whether they believe their way is best or not. If you have been kind enough to have me in your home, I should respect what you do and say. I can leave if I feel that I cannot accept your way of life. You are not the one who should be obligated to change to accommodate my personal feelings. You may do so to some extent to be a good host, but you should not have to do so under threat that I will ransack your house if you do not give in to my desires and demands.

This illustration applies to Muslims worldwide: to those who immigrate to foreign countries and are a minority; to those who are a minority within their own country, as is the case in Thailand where Muslims in the south want autonomy from the rest of the country; and to those who are in countries were Islam is the majority religion. There are conflicts in countries like Algeria in which one group of Muslims is using violence to impose their interpretation of Islam on other Muslims. They have claimed thousands of lives in the process. A case in point would be the 2007 conflict at the Red Mosque in Islamabad. Zealous Muslims wanted to impose a Taliban style of Islam on the rest of Pakistan, a country with an overwhelming Muslim majority, but with differences in ideology.

Some universities in America restrict any display of Christianity, including Christmas cards handed out by instructors, teaching about the Bible, and prayer in class or as part of graduation ceremonies. However, they will go out of their way to designate a special prayer room for their minority Muslim students in order to avoid confrontations. Some universities have even modified their restrooms to provide special areas for the ablutions required before Muslim prayers.

Target stores in Minnesota have accommodated Muslim employees who once worked at the checkout counter by assigning them to new positions. The reason? Muslim employees refused to scan pork products, claiming that pigs are unclean.[1] Such examples of acquiescence are understood as weakness and embolden Muslims to keep pushing for more "rights" until we have become servants in our own store or country.

The goal of these militant Muslims is to make everyone else feel as if they are intolerant and politically incorrect for refusing to bend to all their demands. They are clever at playing to an obliging media, as they pretend to have been abused or taken advantage of. Unfortunately, it seems that the media generally fall for it.

You may have heard of the reaction in France in 2003 to a law forbidding religious attire in schools, including Muslim girls and teachers wearing a hijab (Muslim head cover) in class. It prompted widespread debates over the acceptability of visible displays of religious affiliations.

In 2006, a classroom assistant in England was told she could not work in the classroom with her face veiled because the children could not understand her well without seeing her facial expressions. But again, it was taken as repression of religious freedom.

Also in 2006, British Airways laid off a female employee for wearing a necklace with a cross. They did not want any religious display in the workplace. There is a big difference between having your face covered by a veil and wearing a cross on a necklace. Most people would not be opposed to a Muslim girl wearing a necklace with the star and crescent symbol.

Wearing a veil can be a security risk or, as has happened, can allow a student to cheat by taking an exam in place of another student while hiding behind the veil. The "Chief Examiner's Manual for New York State GED Test Administration" says, "Islamic women may wear burkas (face veils) but in order to check their identity, a female examiner must accompany them to an area where the veil may be lifted and the identity confirmed."[2] A veiled person once pretended to be delivering a package to an office. It turned out to be an explosive device. The person had already left and was unidentifiable because of the face covering. No one was even able to say for sure if it was a woman or a man.

From cradle to grave we are taught—first by our parents, then by the schools, then by life itself—that respect for others should be reciprocal, not one-sided. Crosses have been removed from cemeteries and buildings, and since 1989 the ACLU has been suing to have them removed from war memorials so as not to offend people who do not believe in the cross. Christmas trees and mangers have been removed from public places so as not to offend minority groups. The attitudes and actions of liberals in America have strengthened the hands of Muslims who say they find symbols of Christianity offensive. Go to a Muslim country and ask them not to display their religious symbols because they offend you and you will see what kind of answer you will get.

Being firm in what you believe should not keep you from respecting people who believe differently. In discussions with Muslims, do not make apologies for what you believe. You may need to apologize for not having been as faithful as you should have been to the teachings of the Bible, but do not renounce what you believe is right according to the Bible just to maintain harmony. Christianity should not be forced down anyone's throat, but Muslims should not force their ways upon others either.

I am not writing this to sow resentment toward Muslims or other religious groups but to point out the danger of the policy of appeasement instead of being firm when we need to be firm. Parents who do not give in to all their children's demands will be better off and will have well-behaved and respectful children later on. Both the parents and the children will benefit from common respect. Just as not all children are spoiled and demanding, not all Muslims are demanding either. Some children may be more inclined than others to become demanding and throw fits, but in most cases they become that way because their parents failed to be firm with them or were afraid they might hurt their children's self-esteem by refusing to give in to their demands. We see a similar scenario being played out today with Muslims. Unfortunately, the future of our freedom is at stake, and it may be very difficult to repair the damage that has already been done.

In our many years among Muslims, we have found them for the most part very welcoming and hospitable. Most of them have been very kind to us. I do not attribute that to the fact that they were Muslims, but instead to their cultural background and upbringing. On the other hand, even though we were openly Christian, we did not try to impose our way of life on them. We quietly shared our beliefs with them, comparing what we believe with what they believe, but we did not expect their community to start eating pork because we eat pork or to stop the call to prayer on their loudspeakers because we did not follow Islam. In deference to them, we did not eat pork at our house or in the presence of Muslims.

I assure you that to foreigners the call to prayer and the long chanting of the Qur'an in Arabic over loudspeakers five times a day can become trying, but since we were guests in their country, they could do as they pleased. I was not shy about voicing my opinion and dislike for what I considered annoying noises at all times of the day (especially at 4:30 A.M.), but I did it in a friendly way, not expecting them to change in order to please me. The fact that I did not like to be awakened at 4:30 A.M. by their chanting on loudspeakers did not give me the right to blow up their mosques.

The fact that Islamists in parts of Indonesia, Pakistan, and northern Nigeria burn churches and kill Christians does not give me the right to attack and burn a mosque in my neighborhood, nor to mistreat Muslims living in my country. My Muslim neighbor most likely does not have anything whatsoever to do with what another Muslim in Nigeria, or any other country, is doing to non-Muslims.

Some so-called Christians still call the Jews "Christ-killers." What does a Jew in the twenty-first century have to do with what his ancestors did two thousand years ago? Even at the time of the crucifixion, as bad as it was, thousands of Jews were not present in Jerusalem that day and had no physical part in the crucifixion or the events that led to it. Besides, the whole scenario was pre-planned by God and necessary for the salvation of each one of us.

I have traveled to other parts of the world where Arab Muslims were a majority and found many of the people less than friendly or polite, but again I would attribute that to their traditional culture, not necessarily to Islam. You will find westerners that are very friendly and welcoming and others who are not at all so. Christians should always be welcoming to foreigners and should treat them well. We had wonderful years living among Muslims and felt very much accepted among them, even when living in restrictive Muslim areas. We do not despise Muslims simply because they are Muslims. They are people who can experience and give love like the rest of us can. Some of our dearest friends are Muslims.

Her Majesty Queen Rania Al Abdullah of Jordan on July 6, 2007 wrote:

> Looking back, I learned how to be a Muslim at an early age—not as something separate from daily life, but as something intrinsic to it. I think of my parents' warmth and love; how they helped me, my brother and sister learn to share; and how they taught us to value honesty, humility, charity, and forgiveness. Now a mother myself, I know in my heart that meaning is being made when my children raise their arms for a hug; when we give of ourselves to those less fortunate; when we are reminded, during Ramadan, of the hunger and thirst of those in need.
>
> I cherish these experiences not only because they make me a better Muslim, but because they make me a better person—more grateful, more connected, more aware. And yes, I offer my thanks to God on a prayer mat facing Mecca. But I hope that readers seeking to understand "the true meaning of Islam" will not only focus on how Muslims worship but also on who we are: mothers, fathers, spouses, students, neighbors, friends. People who smile with pride at their child's first step; laugh with friends over the old times; worry about exam results; cry at the sight of our children in pain. People just like you.[3]

Muslims aren't the only minority group that has immigrated to a new country and begun to demand various rights. We need to look at the history of western civilization. Over the centuries, many wars have been fought between Protestants and Catholics, similar to what we now see between Shiites and Sunnis. Many of those wars were vicious. The Thirty Years War (1618–1648) was triggered by religious conflicts between Protestants and Catholics and became one of the most destructive in European history.

In the Peasants' War (1524–1526), both sides committed atrocities and thousands were killed. In England during the 1600s, conflicts between various Protestant groups led to many deaths, massive destruction, and several overthrows of government.

Over the centuries, religion has often been a major source of conflict. Millions have been oppressed, tortured, and killed in the name of God. Today's religious conflicts are not a new thing. A mixture of religion, politics, and the desire for power can be very explosive.

As the world is getting smaller due to faster means of transportation and better communication, it has become a more difficult place to live. We now have to learn to coexist with people who are thousands of miles away and see and do things differently. We would all benefit by trying to better understand each other's culture.

Chapter Eight

Sharing
with Your Friend

Some of you reading this book will remember the days when salesmen went door-to-door peddling their wares. There was no e-Bay or other online shopping in those days. I recall the man who sold for Fuller Brush. He would come to our house from time to time, and my mother would let him in even if she didn't think she needed anything. He would open his display cases and show all his wares. Most of the time my mother would end up buying something after seeing the new products he had to offer. As a kid I remember how much I enjoyed looking at all he had in those cases and wishing my mother would buy it all.

Had my mother kept the salesman out on the front porch and refused to let him in to show what he had to offer, the temptation would not have been there, and she would not have bought anything. It is the same with the Gospel: You have to whet someone's appetite before he will want your product. In order to do this, you may have to enter his house or have that person enter yours. When he sees what you have to offer, he may become interested. But if you leave him out on the front porch, he probably will never become a customer.

I have seen churches who claim that they pray for Muslims to come to know Jesus, but their approach is more or less along this line of thinking: "The church is here. We have been in this same spot for years. If they want to come, they know where we are." Probably 99.9 percent of them have never had a Muslim cross their threshold. Why would a Muslim who drives by a church building every day on his way to work want to go in for a Sunday service?

First of all, which church would he choose since there is such a smorgasbord of churches? Where would he start? Free-Will Baptist, Southern Baptist, Assemblies of God, Pentecostal Holiness, Lutheran, Catholic, Presbyterian, Church of Christ—you name it. They are all there for him to choose from.

What would he do after he enters the church building? Most people would probably stare at him as if he were an alien from Mars, especially if he were dressed a bit differently and if he took off his shoes in respect for the house of God. Imagine what would happen if during the prayer time, he stepped into the aisle and prostrated himself before God. He would probably be told in no uncertain terms that this was not a mosque and if he could not behave properly he should leave. Some churches might even call 911, thinking he was probably a terrorist about to blow up the place. Perhaps this is a bit unfair since some churches would know better, but many would not.

Most Muslims will never enter a church unless they are accompanied by a friend who has invited them and can introduce them to people and explain what is going on. This leads to the big question: How can we become friends with Muslims so someday we can invite them to church with us?

First of all, inviting a Muslim to church might not be the best idea, at least not at the beginning of your friendship. He would probably be very uncomfortable and if his Muslim friends or family were to find out that he had been to church, he could be in big trouble. I know that some Christians would be in trouble with their church if it were known that they went to a mosque to please a Muslim who invited them.

It is sad to say, but your Muslim friend might be offended by some of the things he would probably see in church, such as the way some people dress or act. Muslims believe that God is holy and therefore people should dress and behave with utmost respect and reverence in his house. For example, they believe that women should dress modestly in the house of God, which includes not wearing low-cut dresses, let alone mini-skirts or short shorts.

Instead of inviting a Muslim coworker or acquaintance to church, let me suggest that you begin by trying to make friends with him and his family. Do not try to build friendship with just one individual, isolating him from his family. That could be regarded with suspicion. Try to meet the entire family if you can.

You do not need to be a preacher to share your faith with Muslims; however, you have to be a true believer or they may see right through you. What if they see that you yourself do not put into practice some of the very things the Bible teaches? Remember, you do not want to be a stumbling block or be the cause of Muslims turning away from Jesus. Could a Muslim's view of Jesus be distorted because you are in the way? If you seriously want to share your faith with Muslims, you may first have to "clean up your own house."

Zacchaeus was a short man as we read in Luke 19:1–9. He had to climb a tree in order to see Jesus when he came down the street surrounded by a crowd. A speaker once pointed out that the reason Zacchaeus could not see Jesus was probably because the twelve apostles—those big brawny men—were surrounding Jesus and blocking the view. The speaker warned everyone to be careful not to be the ones blocking the view of Jesus. Muslims see Jesus through the lives of people who claim to be his disciples, much more than through what those people have to say about him.

If you do not already know someone who is Muslim, try to find a Muslim family living in your area. Find a way to get acquainted with them. When I was in an area where I did not really know any Muslims, guess what I did in order to meet some of them? I went to the mosque on Friday at their prayer time. There I met some very friendly Muslims. After prayers were over, they all shook hands with me and invited me to join some of the men at 10 o'clock that night for coffee and donuts at the back of the mosque. I did return, and we had a great time. They asked me many questions about Christianity, and I inquired about their faith, as well.

Later on, I invited the Imam of that mosque to a church where I was teaching a class about Islam. Not only did he come, but several other men from the mosque joined him. I had him speak to the class. He did a great job. He was a very articulate Egyptian doctor. Later, Daena and I invited him and his wife to our house for a meal. They came and we had a pleasant evening together. Perhaps you could do something similar.

Do not pretend to be someone you are not. Be honest. Before you try to "preach" to your Muslim friend, get to know him better. You can ask questions about his family, his background, what his hobbies are, where he works, and what country he was from originally. If he is an immigrant, ask about customs in his country. You will see that it can be very interesting, and you will learn much you did not know.

Try to compliment him about things in his family, find good things to say about his country. Eventually, you can bring the conversation to Islam and ask him questions about his religion. What does it mean to him? What are some of their big religious holidays? What do they do on those days? What are the special foods they eat? Do they wear different clothes for those celebrations? Ask him how he feels about being here, how people relate to him, what things he found the most difficult to adjust to, what changes he would like to see. No matter how you feel about it, avoid criticizing his home country, their ways of doing things, and his religion.

Be prepared for a long-term relationship, whether your new friend shows any interest at first in what you say about Jesus or not. Do not ask all the above questions at one sitting. Muslims are not stupid either. They will know if your sole purpose for inviting them was to preach to them. Nobody likes to be used that way. Someone living in a predominantly Muslim country told me that Muslims were welcomed at his house if they wanted to hear about Christianity and do Bible studies with him. However, if all they wanted to do was to visit and practice their English with him, he had no time for that. He felt that all they were doing was taking advantage of him. I do not agree with that.

What Christians call "the family of God" has become more like an exclusive club. Many people spend so much time at church and doing things with other Christians that they have become worthless at reaching out to non-believers. They are so "holy" that they have to stay away from non-Christians to avoid being corrupted by them. Going to church on

Sunday for Sunday school, then the worship service and evening service, participating in the Monday night Bible study, attending the Wednesday night prayer meeting, being part of the choir, serving on the board of elders or deacons, leading a youth group...

All that is good, but my opinion is that churches should try to set limits on how much time any member can spend in "church-related activities." In large churches, this trend can become even more pronounced. Some mega-churches have become like large country clubs. They offer a large range of activities and services, such as golfing, basketball, softball, fishing trips, excursions for all ages around the country and overseas, aerobics, health classes, money management classes, marriage enrichment seminars, plus bookstores, cafes and restaurants... You name it, they've got it. Members can easily spend their entire social life in the security of church-related activities. They live in a sanitized cocoon.

It is good to fellowship with other believers, and everyone needs the support of other Christians. However, our main goal as believers should be to help others outside the church and be salt and light in the world. "You are the salt of the earth. But if the salt loses its saltiness, how can it be made salty again? It is no longer good for anything, except to be thrown out and trampled by men. You are the light of the world. A city on a hill cannot be hidden" (Matthew 5:13–14). We are not saved to warm church pews. The missionary statesman Oswald Smith wrote that a church's size should not be measured by how many people are present on Sunday, but by how many people it sends out to reach the lost.

It is sad to say, but the lives of many Christians are pretty much tasteless to "sinners," and their light does not shine very far outside the four walls of their church. If your life is "salty," it will make people thirsty and as Jesus said, "If anyone is thirsty, let him come to me and drink" (John 7:37).

This is not intended to be a course on how to share your faith with Muslims, but to give you ideas on how to start a friendship and help you "think outside the box." Many good books have treated at length the subject of sharing your faith, giving Scriptures relating to the Qur'an and suggesting possible guidelines to follow. You don't need to spend years studying about Islam before you can share your faith with its adherents, but it is good to know the basics of their belief. Reading *How to Respond—Muslims*[1] by Ernest Hawn would be a good place to start. It is a short, well-written book that would give you a good basis to work from. If you want a more extensive study of Islam, *Ishmael My Brother*[2] compiled by Anne Cooper is a very good book designed to be used for group study.

Chapter Nine

CULTURAL BLUNDERS

"I WOULD LOVE TO GO OVER THERE and teach those natives."

People have often told me they would like to go to Africa or Asia where my wife and I have worked and teach "those natives." I have always tried to give an evasive answer so as not to insult them, but I have often wondered what they would teach "those natives." Besides the condescending attitude their description of local populations reveals, most people cannot effectively teach those of another cultural background without first taking time to learn about—and often learn from—"those natives." Unfortunately, many of these would-be teachers who do go overseas make blunders and at times say things that are insensitive and/or offending to their listeners.

Some westerners do nothing but criticize their host culture, always comparing it to the way things are done "back home." That attitude does more to tear down than to build up. They complain about the food, the roads, the way people dress, or the way the government functions or doesn't. These people are miserable and because they are so frustrated by their host culture they would be better off returning to their home country. They forget that there are a lot of frustrating things back home, too. The difference is that the annoyances they face at home are things they are accustomed to and therefore do not notice as much—polluted air, rush-hour traffic, junk food, immorality on television and in movies, family breakups, and other ills that wreak havoc in their own culture.

Instead of looking for negatives to gripe about, they should appreciate the positives in their host culture. Along with the frustrating things, our family has found plenty of good things in Africa and Asia—things we would like to see implemented in our home countries. Africans and Asians have a rich heritage that can enrich ours as well.

I enjoy observing people and have been amazed at the cultural differences that exist even within our own society. People with similar backgrounds and levels of education tend to gravitate toward each other. It's difficult for people with lower levels of education to befriend doctors, lawyers, and CEOs. They have little in common. A marriage between a surgeon and a person with little education from a low-income family will almost inevitably encounter difficulties even if both are very much in love.

When the doctor has friends over, the spouse will have difficulty making conversation and developing and enjoying the relationships. By the same token, the educated partner will likely be uncomfortable with the spouse's friends. It's a bit like a young computer engineer trying to explain nanotechnology to his grandmother. She probably would not find it very interesting and would quickly tire of the subject. Of course there are always exceptions, but this is generally the case.

To better illustrate the impact that the introduction of elements from one culture into another can have, here are some examples drawn from our experiences with assorted people groups in Africa and Asia.

It is not uncommon to hear people say: "Africans do this or do that" or "Asians do it this way or that way." While there may be room to generalize cultural trends, African and Asian practices can differ considerably from one ethnic group to another and from one region or country to another.

In Africa and Asia, I was frequently asked what tribe we were from, and the person asking would inevitably be surprised to hear that we do not have tribes among white North Americans. Tribal and ethnic loyalties can be very strong. They have been and still are the cause of many conflicts and even full-scale wars. Intermarriage between different tribes, ethnic groups, and even between different castes within the same group is still the exception, not unlike interracial marriage in the West.

Different tribal groups within an African country, and even more so across the entire continent, differ from each other more than most North

Americans do. Part of the reason for this is that transportation and communication were very limited and still are in many areas. On the world stage, an extreme example of this is found in Papua New Guinea. A very mountainous nation about the size of California, it has 5.3 million inhabitants divided into approximately 1,000 tribes that speak 860 distinct languages.

Many of the people we worked with in Africa had never been more than perhaps fifty miles (eighty kilometers) from home and a fair number not even that far. Millions of Africans do not have access to television; short-wave radios are often their only window to the outside world. For example, although the Dogon people of Mali are from one ethnic group, their dialects vary from one village to another, despite having as little as twenty-five miles (forty kilometers) between them. This comes from the fact that on foot, twenty-five miles is a long way, and you do not get to see each other often. Over the years, the dialect in each village has changed to the point that people from different villages can't understand each other.

The Senoufo ethnic groups that straddle Mali, Burkina Faso and Côte d'Ivoire (Ivory Coast) speak a wide range of Senoufo dialects. A Senoufo from Kadiolo can barely understand his fellow Senoufo from Sikasso, only sixty-two miles (one hundred kilometers) away. Only about one word in five is the same. They use a completely different language, Jula, to communicate with one another. Jula is very similar to Bambara, the language of Mali's largest tribe. The word actually means "trader," as indeed Jula is the trade language used to communicate with those from distant areas of their own and surrounding tribes. As a result, when Senoufos from different areas meet in the market, they use Jula instead of communicating in their mother tongue because they can both understand the trade language.

While we lived in Mali, a large Christian organization with offices in Europe and America sent prerecorded radio shows on family life to be aired on local African stations. The material was free of charge and since local radio stations often suffered from a lack of material to air, they played the imported presentations. Most of the material in these programs was not applicable to the culture of the listeners in Africa. Some of it was even considered immoral and offensive (such as the advice to show affection to your wife in front of your children).

Some of the more educated listeners followed the programs with curiosity simply to learn about the differences in our respective cultures, knowing that very little of the content actually applied to their family situation. Despite being sincere in their effort to benefit the Africans, that Christian organization failed to be aware of the cultural differences between westerners and Africans. Their effort to reach out and help with advice on family life was therefore rendered ineffective. Family values are often quite different from culture to culture. They can also vary considerably from one subgroup to another within our western culture.

The Pokot people of northwest Kenya are a pastoral tribe, so their livelihood revolves around their cows, goats, and camels. They grow some corn and millet, but the harshness of the land, combined with erratic rainfall, makes agriculture very difficult. They live off the milk from their animals and drink some of the blood of their cattle during the dry season.

The lifestyle of the Pokot in the early 1980s would have appeared primitive to our western eyes. Men wore only a piece of cloth the size of a twin bedsheet tied around their waist or over one shoulder, and at times nothing at all. Women wore home-tanned cow hides to cover their lower body and upper legs, rarely covering their breasts.

A Christian organization started a work there and a few Pokot converted to Christianity. A young couple, Loitaluk and Chepkukat, were the first Christians to be married. (Names have been changed to protect people's privacy.) The missionaries, biased by their western mindset, wanted to teach them the basic elements of a "Christian wedding." They didn't have a "proper" church building yet, so they used a dilapidated grass-roofed shelter that was used for food distribution and decorated it for the occasion with colorful balloons. A white shirt, dark slacks, leather shoes and tie were acquired for the groom and tennis shoes, a long white skirt, white blouse, and veil for the bride. In the ceremony the bride and groom exchanged vows and rings. This was supposed to be a "Christian wedding," complete with a nice three-tiered layer cake baked by one of the missionary wives for the reception.

I was newly arrived in Africa at that time. The ceremony, while I found it amusing, raised questions for me. What part of that ceremony was "Christian"? Does the Bible give us an example of a "Christian wedding"? Apart from the prayers for the new couple asked in Jesus' name, to me all the rest was nothing more than a ceremony steeped in western tradition, having very little to do with Christianity. In Pokot culture, the bride would have normally worn a braided leather bracelet as an indication that she was married. Now, as a Christian Pokot, she was wearing a ring. What makes a ring more spiritual than a bracelet?

It would probably have been a more meaningful ceremony and would certainly have been more culturally appropriate if the missionaries had taken time beforehand to find out how traditional Pokot wedding ceremonies are performed. Of course, the elements of their traditional ceremonies that were contrary to biblical teaching—such as spirit-worship— would have had to be removed. A Christian dimension could have been incorporated in their place. Instead, the missionaries conveyed the message that traditional weddings are not proper for Christians. A major problem with this message is the practicality and sustainability of it. How can a people living a hand-to-mouth existence afford on their own to purchase the necessary trappings for a "Christian wedding"?

Here is an example of a more complicated and difficult to foresee situation. That same mission organization had built several elementary schools. Since the people were semi-nomadic, very few of the children had ever been to school. The mission agency built a boarding school so the children could attend classes and gave the children (only boys at the beginning) school uniforms, fed them three meals a day, and had them sleep in dormitories.

For children who had never worn western clothes and did not always have something to eat at home, these were luxuries. Each boy was given a bright yellow shirt and blue shorts that had been sent from the USA. Most of the boys did not know how to put on the shirt. At suppertime, as usual, everyone sat on the ground to eat. Since the children did not want to dirty the seat of their new shorts, they simply pulled them partly down and sat on their bare bottoms.

Eventually, several families agreed to let a daughter attend school, but the others had to remain at home to help their parents. Normally when boys were six or seven years of age, they herded goats, and cows. But now, instead of herding cattle, many boys—anywhere from six to fifteen when they started first grade—were in school.

This was all very nice until the time came that they were done with grade school. The area had no source of paid employment for them, and now that they were "educated" and had tasted the "good life" in boarding school, they did not want to follow in their parents' footsteps and live the harsh life of nomadic cattle herders. They wanted office jobs.

One by one they left the area and joined the thousands of others who lived in slums surrounding large cities hoping to find jobs. The students' rejection of their traditional way of life angered their parents and made many of them regret ever having agreed to send their children to school.

Another unforeseen difficulty arose when it came time for them to get married. In that culture, the groom's family had to give the bride's family a certain number of cattle, and possibly other livestock, as part of the engagement and marriage ritual. In good years, this bride price could be as high as thirty-five cows plus some goats and a few donkeys. Often, young men would get part of the bride price by rustling cattle from neighboring tribes during armed cattle raids. Of course, school had kept them from that traditional tribal practice. These young men, having been in school for eight or ten years and not having cared for their families' livestock, had no cattle for the bride price. Their parents refused to give them cattle, saying, "You chose to go to school and did not help us herd or care for the cattle. Now do not expect us to give you animals for the bride price."

No one would have thought or argued that teaching people to read or offering an education was a bad thing. Certainly the education of young people is important. The problem was that the realities of the local tribal culture had once more been left out of the equation. This created problems the missionaries had not foreseen.

Chapter Ten

WHAT A TANGLED WEB!

ISLAM ALLOWS A MAN TO HAVE up to four wives but stipulates that he cannot favor one over the other. He has to treat them all equally. Not all Muslims approve of polygamy. We have known many who are against it. Moreover, polygamy is not confined to Islam. Most, if not all, African ethnic groups accept polygamy, whether they are Muslims or not. Unlike Muslims, non-Muslim groups generally do not set a limit on how many wives a man can have. We have often seen African men with five or six wives. The practice is declining due in part to the fact that more girls and young women are getting an education and object strongly to being a third or fourth wife.

Economics are a factor as well. As more people move away from the farmland to the big city, it has become more difficult to house and support several wives. Many well-to-do Africans have a young, better educated wife who lives with them in the city and several other wives who are out in the country taking care of farms with their children.

As you can imagine, solving family and marriage conflicts with four or more wives and perhaps more than twenty children, is quite different than with one wife and two kids. The suggestions often given by marriage counselors in the western world (such as leaving your children with a babysitter once a week and taking your wife to a nice restaurant so you can have a quiet time to talk together or even going on a second honeymoon) take a very different dimension when you have several wives and so many children. Somehow, taking your four wives out for a nice meal once a week or taking all of them on a second honeymoon sounds like more trouble than it is worth.

In Mali, our next-door neighbor had three wives and twenty-one children. Our landlord had four wives and twenty-four children. I have never heard of them taking the family out to a restaurant for a night out. You may wonder how a man can support all those wives with so many kids. Most men do not; instead, each wife, along with her children, works on the farm or sells produce, handmade baskets, or mats at the market or she has some other kind of business or trade to help support herself and often her husband as well.

You may ask: "But why would a girl accept to become a fourth wife?" Volumes would have to be written to explain the complexities of polygamous marriages. They vary a lot among the different ethnic groups all over the world, but in many cases the girls or young women (and sometimes even the young men) do not have much choice as to whom they will marry. The extended family, often after lengthy and complicated negotiations, decides for them.

Frequently, marriages are used to create or strengthen bonds between families or clans. Young women are sometimes "sold" to the highest bidder. At other times, they are more or less traded between families living in a certain area. "We gave you one of our daughters in marriage two years ago; it is now your turn to give us one of your daughters in marriage for our son." For some, the bride price is mostly livestock, for others it will be livestock along with rice or corn, some clothes and some cash. Bride prices vary according to the economy of the region, the wealth of the family, their position in society, the education of the young woman and whether or not she has proven (before being married) that she can bear children. At times the bride price can be paid in installments.

The selection of the wife for a young man often involves long discussions among relatives. Western-style dating or courtship are rare. If a young man is getting married, the father and uncles may all pitch in for the bride price (the situation will be different for an older man adding another wife). In this way, the new wife is not only the concern of the young man, but also of the extended family. This will make it much more difficult for him to decide to divorce later on if he should ever be inclined to do so. The whole extended family will step in and say, "Hey, we paid part of the bride price for that woman. You cannot send her back to her family."

If the husband dies, the family of the husband will give her in marriage to another male member of the extended family since she is part of their family now—not her parents' family. Once again, she will not decide on her own whom she will marry next. She may not even have a say in choosing whether to remarry or not. In our eyes, it seems like the woman is treated more as if she were a piece of property or livestock than a human being with feelings of her own.

Since the whole family was involved in the transaction to choose the wife and paid part of the bride price, the children from that marriage also belong to the extended family, not just to the immediate parents. It is common and accepted for relatives living some distance away to take one of the children from a young family because they need help at home. Sometimes it is a boy to help on the farm or a young girl to help with household chores or the care of a grandmother, etc. That child might live the rest of his/her growing years with that distant relative. It is hard for us to understand how parents could send away one of their children and not see him or her again for years, if ever. In Mali, children are often given to wealthier relatives in Côte d'Ivoire (Ivory Coast) to help in their home or on coffee or cocoa plantations.

Although most—if not all—ethnic groups in Africa place high importance on the extended family and communal priorities, different ethnic groups maintain their extended families in varying ways, with varying traditions of marriage arrangements. The Senoufo people of southern Mali, for example, do not pay their complete bride price in the form of cattle, cloth, jewelry, grain and/or money as many ethnic groups do. Instead, the Senoufo have a tradition of working for the bride price, similar to Jacob in the Old Testament, who worked a total of fourteen years for Leah and Rachel.

Marriages are arranged while children are still quite young. If a family has a young son, for example, they will negotiate with another family for a girl to marry that boy when the two become old enough to wed. The relatives of the boy—the father, older brothers, and uncles—will work the land several weeks per year for the family of the girl. Which girl in particular in that family will be given may not have been decided yet, but one of the daughters will eventually be given to the other family as a bride.

The relatives of the boy may work for girls of more than one family for that boy. Therefore, assuming they have enough manpower, they may cultivate the land of several families in order to have several wives for the son. The more sons a man has, the more cultivating has to be done to acquire wives. They may only be able to afford one wife for each son until the sons are older and can arrange to marry more wives on their own.

Moussa and Miriam were a young Senoufo couple. His father was the chief of a small village in Mali. Moussa and his wife converted from Islam to Christianity and now wanted to live by Christian standards. Unfortunately, those standards conflicted with Senoufo culture and traditions. One day, Moussa told me that a new girl had moved into their extended family compound. She was perhaps fourteen or fifteen years old. The father had not told the sons yet who would have her for a wife, but Moussa, because of his position as an older son, feared she may be assigned to him. Being a Christian now, he did not want to take a second wife, but he knew his refusal would not go well with his father and uncles.

Moussa had been right; the girl was for him. The father was upset with him for not wanting a second wife. He wanted Moussa to have a good standing in the community, and having many wives increases one's importance. There was also the fact that the family had already worked for that girl and did not want all their investment to be lost because of a stubborn son with a new religion. Fortunately for Moussa, he had several younger brothers, and the girl was eventually given in marriage to one of them, but in the process, Moussa lost respect and his position in the family hierarchy.

Moussa's father and uncles, who had negotiated the marriage and wanted him to have a second wife, were a mixture of animist and Muslim. Many Muslims are considered part of what is called "folk Islam," a mixture of Islam and local traditional religions. A similar blending often happens with Christians, so the term could also apply to them. We could call it "folk Christianity." These people have more or less added Islam or Christianity to their ancestral beliefs and traditions and try to make the best of it all.

For example, a Catholic woman who worked in a hotel in Cotonou, Benin once told some friends and me that going to church was good but that a person also needs to wear charms and offer sacrifices to protect the family against evil spirits. She said that the church gave good teachings and hope for the afterlife, but that it was powerless to protect them from illnesses and other woes.

You can see how Christian teachings would clash in many cases with the cultural tradition of the Senoufo or many other people groups. There are no easy answers to these complicated situations. We know that children should respect and submit to their parents, but to what extent should they do so when that obedience conflicts with other Christian principles?

What do you do when a man becomes a believer but already has several wives? From what has already been mentioned concerning the complicated bride price system and extended family relationships, you can imagine how this could put a family in a difficult position. Should he continue living as before with all his wives and children? If he keeps only the first wife, what will he do with the others and all the children? What about his responsibility to take his brother's wives and children when the brother dies in an accident or from illness?

We knew a man in Kenya who had sixteen wives. Most of them he had inherited from his brothers who had died in cattle raids. Being a single widowed mother is not really an option for women since they need to remain connected and an active part of an extended family network, a social system that is vitally important to their culture.

German author Walter Trobisch, who worked in Cameroon for many years, wrote several excellent books on the subject of polygamy and arranged marriages. Two in particular are *My Wife Made Me a Polygamist*[1] *and I Loved a Girl/ I Loved a Young Man.*[2] I would strongly recommend reading his books on the subject.

How would you like to be a Christian marriage counselor and have men come to you who have some of the problems inherent in polygamous marriages? Here are some of the issues you would have to deal with:

Youssouf does not get along with one of his wives; Adama's wives are jealous of each other and keep quarrelling among themselves; one of Brahima's wives has been unfaithful; Daouda's brother died and left him with three more wives and twelve kids; Lotuboy's teenage son is refusing to marry the bride that was chosen for him by the family; one of Boubacar's daughters ran away because she does not want to marry the man who has already paid the bride price for her; the wives are upset because Sheick wants to take one more wife (a younger and good-looking girl who has gone to school, but can't even cook).

Islam allows for four wives, but what does the Bible say about polygamy? We know that God created Adam and Eve, not Adam, Eve, Miriam and Rachel. So we may deduce that God intended man to have one wife, not many wives. But, in the Old Testament we see plenty of examples of polygamy, even among our favorite kings and patriarchs such as Abraham, Jacob, David, Solomon, etc. We also see all the headaches and trouble it brought them. God did not necessarily rebuke them for taking more than one wife.

On the contrary, in Genesis 38 we see that God put Onan, Judah's son, to death because he refused to take his older brother's wife and give her children after his brother had died. Deuteronomy 25:5 says: "If brothers are living together and one of them dies without a son, his widow must not marry outside the family. Her husband's brother shall take her and marry her and fulfill the duty of a brother-in-law to her." We see in verses 7–10 that serious repercussions came on the brother who refused to follow this rule.

Mohammed lived in a time when polygamy was the norm, so it is not surprising that he approved of it. Obviously he was aware of the difficulties polygamy can bring, so he tried to set some limits and certain rules to be followed, such as not having more than four wives at the same time and treating all of them equally. Unfortunately, it seems that none of these rules applied to him. Mohammed had some fourteen wives during his lifetime, many of them wed to form alliances with various groups, as was common at that time. He was very familiar with the difficulties of polygamy, including jealousy and quarreling in the family.

What a Tangled Web!

What does the New Testament have to say on the subject? The four gospels do not make any mention of Jesus ever referring to polygamy. Jesus had a lot to say against divorce and remarriage, teachings that are ignored by many of his followers today.

The only possible references to polygamy in the New Testament are found in Paul's epistles. In 1 Timothy 3:2 and in Titus 1:6, Paul says that an elder should be the husband of but one wife. He says that along with many other criteria for choosing elders. Apparently many men became Christians after they already had more than one wife.

In our western society today, churches would probably never dream of electing a man with multiple wives as an elder, but in many cases they are much less stringent about the rest of the attributes Paul required. Neither Peter nor any of the other New Testament writers mentioned polygamy. Families apparently came to Christ with whatever marital configuration they had, but monogamy was what was taught.

Although we can see that the New Testament talks about a man's relationship with "his wife" and not "his wives" (Ephesians 5:22–33), we should not be too quick or harsh in passing judgment on polygamy itself. We must be careful not to let our cultural views get in the way of seeing God's views. Can we say that our ways are perfect? Westerners generally do not approve of having several wives at the same time but often accept people having them in a series, a sequential form of polygamy.

Think of the high rate of cohabitation or divorce and remarriage in our society, even among so-called Christians. A friend told me recently that in the small church he attends, they have three women who have each been married three times. In a polygamous family, the children know their parents and all the co-wives are their "mothers." In the western world, you have custody battles and children often are shuttled between one household and another, making a very unstable environment for raising children. We also have numerous one-parent households.

Things are changing in the developing world also. The coming of television, videos, Internet, and greater access to news from the outside world is rapidly affecting cultures, even among devout Muslim families. Video rental places can now be found even in remote villages. Teenagers there, just like here, desire change; they do not want to follow the old ways. Sometimes it is for the better, but unfortunately, they tend to be better at adopting the bad aspects of our culture instead of the good ones.

Men, who in the past were the head of the family and held total authority, now see that authority being eroded by ideas coming from outside their culture. As you would expect, they resent that and in many cases are trying to reestablish their authority. This is in part why there has been a revival of Islamic traditions in many countries. The older people are afraid of the new ways and see them as contrary to their faith and an erosion of their traditional values.

When someone approaches people from another culture and tries to teach them what he thinks to be better ways of living or doing things, expecting them to abandon their old ways, he needs to be prepared to have something that will work to replace the old customs. He cannot just create a vacuum. Finding a replacement for their old traditions may turn out to be difficult. By trying to solve one problem, he may end up creating another one—and often several more. Religions, old or new, always have a big influence on culture, and old ways always die hard.

In the Old Testament, God spoke from Mount Sinai to the Israelites. Moses went up the mountain and received the Ten Commandments. Although God did reveal himself to his people, he was distant. In the New Testament, God came down to live with us in the form of his son, Jesus. Jesus took on a human body and could fully identify with the culture around him. In the same way, we need to live with the people and learn to understand their culture before trying to introduce new ways.

As Paul explains so well in 1 Corinthians 13, it is not how smart we are or how superior we may think we are, or how hard we work that counts, but how much we love. "And now these three things remain: faith, hope and love. But the greatest of these is love" (v. 13). In sharing his faith, a Christian should always be mindful of the intricate social network in which traditional peoples live.

Conclusion

"'I AM THE WAY AND THE TRUTH AND THE LIFE. No one comes to the Father except through me. If you really knew me, you would know my Father as well...' Philip said, 'Lord, show us the Father and that will be enough for us.' Jesus answered: 'Don't you know me, Philip, even after I have been among you such a long time? Anyone who has seen me has seen the Father. How can you say, "Show us the Father"?'" (John 14:6–9).

After spending three years walking with Jesus, listening to his teaching, and seeing the miracles he performed, the disciples still could not fully grasp his divinity. We see this also in Luke 24:13–35, where Jesus joined two of his disciples who were walking on the road to Emmaus after the crucifixion. "And beginning with Moses and all the Prophets, he explained to them what was said in all the Scriptures concerning himself" (v. 27). Jesus needed to go back all the way to the time of Moses and explain the Scriptures to them before they could understand who he truly was. Jesus could well have said, "I am fed up with you. Can't you ever understand anything? Why can't you understand the Torah's teaching? How is it possible that you do not see that I am the fulfillment of what was prophesied in the Torah and the Prophets?"

Jesus had to miraculously open the eyes of their hearts and minds before they could grasp that reality. "When he was at the table with them, he took the bread, gave thanks, broke it and began to give it to them. Then their eyes were opened and they recognized him, and he disappeared from their sight. They asked each other, 'Were not our hearts burning within us while he talked with us on the road and opened the Scriptures to us?'" (Luke 24:30–32).

Jesus' followers were good people, and they loved God (like many Muslims today), but they were blinded by their "cultural eyes." Things had to fit into their cultural mold and preconceptions to make sense. They could not think outside the box. It took a miracle, the work of the Holy Spirit, to change their hearts and minds. Aren't we the same way today? Isn't it difficult at times for us to think outside the box? We are comfortable working within our cultural world, but when we venture out of what is familiar we are out of our security zone, and we fear the unknown. Unfortunately, many people do not dare step out of their cultural box. To them, the rest of the world should shape up and fit *their* mold.

It is not only difficult for most people to think outside the box, at times we are also guilty of trying to make God fit inside *our* box. Instead of searching to understand what God actually meant for everyone in a particular passage in the Scriptures, we more or less intentionally interpret it the way we think it should be and then try to fit God into our box so it will fit our theology. We go on saying: "The Bible says…," but did God truly say that, or is that what we think he should have meant by what he said?

Jesus came for everyone, not just for the "more enlightened" westerners. Jesus' teachings are as applicable to low-income people as to the well-to-do, to the uneducated as to the scholar, to the city dweller as to the peasant or nomad, to people with all shades of skin color, to the Asian, Indian, Hispanic, Arab, or European.

The problem did not end with the two disciples on the road to Emmaus. As we read the book of Acts and the epistles, we can see that the cultural issues kept coming up again and again. Most of the Jews at that time who accepted Jesus' teachings believed that Gentiles should conform to Jewish culture as part of becoming Christians.

I suggest you carefully read the letter Paul wrote to the Galatians. Paul fought the religious and cultural narrowness of his time. But even today, with the Scriptures as our example, we still have to struggle with cultural issues. If Paul were here today, he would again say, "I fear for you, that somehow I have wasted my efforts on you" (Galatians 4:11). Christians read the Scriptures but sometimes fail to see how they are applicable to everyday life. It is comparable to a high school student who studies algebra because it is a required subject to graduate, but fails to see how he can ever use it in his life. Some Christians read portions of the Bible as they would a required subject, but fail to see how it applies to their lives.

"No one lights a lamp and hides it in a jar or puts it under a bed. Instead, he puts it on a stand, so that those who come in can see the light" (Luke 8:16). It is unfortunate that the light of the Gospel has been "put under the bed" as far as certain people groups are concerned. It is estimated that there are about two hundred million nomadic livestock herders in the world today and most of them are Muslims.

They have been made to feel that Christianity is not for them since Christians are expected to be in a church building on Sundays. But as nomadic herders, they cannot do that, so they follow Islam because Muslims do not have to be in a mosque to recite their prayers. These nomads cannot leave their nomadic lifestyle, inherited from their ancestors, to become sedentary farmers or city dwellers. For most of them it is not a question of choice, but of survival.

Millions of people who were already polygamous before they heard the Gospel have been made to feel that Christianity was not for them, since Christianity does not approve of polygamy. Some church groups have been more receptive and accept families who were polygamous before becoming believers, but there is still a lot of division on that issue. In many churches, polygamists are considered second-rate Christians and are refused baptism and communion. Church leaders have failed to recognize that Jesus invited the people to come to him as they were, but then taught them to live differently.

Unfortunately, Christians often expect unbelievers to behave like believers before considering them worthy to even hear the message of salvation. They want Muslims to understand that it is not necessary to take their shoes off before entering God's house, or to pray five times a day, or to fast during the month of Ramadan, and so on before they even come to know the freedom there is in Christ. Actually there is nothing in the Bible that forbids taking off one's shoes before entering a place of worship or praying five times per day or fasting for a month each year. Those things are optional and have a lot to do with culture.

As a matter of fact, in Exodus 3:5 when God talked to Moses from the burning bush he said, "Take off your sandals for the place where you are standing is holy ground." In Joshua 5:14–15 when the commander of the Lord's army appeared to Joshua prior to the fall of Jericho we read: "Then Joshua fell facedown to the ground in reverence, and asked him, 'What message does my Lord have for his servant?' The commander of the LORD's army replied, 'Take off your sandals, for the place where you are standing is holy.'"

The Old Testament has many examples showing that it was customary to fall prostrate before dignitaries and even more so before God. Still today, in many parts of Africa and Asia, people remove their shoes before entering someone's house. Keeping your shoes on is a sign of disrespect. By contrast, where I grew up, for an adult to take off his shoes in the house of strangers was considered rude and disrespectful.

We can argue that the things just mentioned are not essentials since we are saved by grace and not by works, but certainly they are not sinful either. Perhaps it would be good for many Christians to be more respectful in church. I am sure we could all benefit from fasting more regularly and praying five times per day.

For Muslims, taking off their shoes before entering a mosque is a "must," but I have also been in some churches where the Doxology is sung every Sunday and it has become so much a part of the service that without it, the service would not seem complete. For those congregations, singing the Doxology is a "must." You would think that one of the commandments is, "Thou Shalt Sing the Doxology Every Sunday."

I have heard of an African Bible college student who had just graduated and was leading a Sunday morning service. He was nervous and inverted the order in which the church was accustomed to reciting the Apostles' Creed, the Lord's Prayer, and singing the Doxology. He was reprimanded by older preachers who asked him what he had been taught in Bible college.

In Matthew 23:13, Jesus says: "Woe to you, teachers of the law and Pharisees, you hypocrites! You shut the kingdom of heaven in men's faces.

You yourselves do not enter, nor will you let those enter who are trying to." If Jesus were here today and were speaking at a national church convention, he might use much the same language.

Christians need to reconsider their way of looking at the Scriptures and see if, because of their inability to see with another person's cultural eyes, they have been guilty of "shutting the kingdom of heaven in men's faces." May God help us and forgive us for our past mistakes.

The content of this book will have certainly "stepped on some people's toes." In some areas of Asia, literally stepping on someone's toes is considered terribly offensive. A man could kill for that. Aren't you glad this is not the case in all cultures? Thank you for reading on even if you may have felt offended and pricked. We all still have a lot to learn.

Jesus, himself, says in John 17:3: "Now this is eternal life: that they may *know* you, the only true God, and Jesus Christ, whom you have sent" (italics mine). It does not say that eternal life depends on the form of the worship service, whether you use one cup or many cups for communion, whether you sing the Doxology or not, whether you keep your shoes on or take them off, etc. The important thing is to *know* God and Jesus Christ whom he has sent. Do you really *know* God and Jesus Christ whom he has sent? Do you really *know* him well enough to introduce him to others as he should be introduced? Paul said, "I want to know Christ and the power of his resurrection and the fellowship of sharing in his sufferings, becoming like him in his death, and so, somehow, to attain to the resurrection from the dead" (Philippians 3:10–11). Paul *knew* Jesus, not only from what he had heard about him, but through having suffered with him. Paul had a close and personal relationship with Jesus and became one of the best communicators of the Gospel the world has ever known.

We also need to walk closely with Jesus and, perhaps to suffer with him, in order to become better communicators of the Gospel. Where there is no pain, there is no gain. Are we willing to "suffer" in order that Muslims might be introduced to Jesus and come to *know* Him?

Light is stronger than darkness. The instant a light is turned on in a room, no matter how dark the room was, the darkness disappears and the light reigns. Imagine entering a room with no windows where complete darkness prevails. You locate the light switch, and then pull the door shut behind you. You stand there in the dark and flip the light switch, but nothing happens. It is still pitch black. What will come to your mind? Will you stand there wondering why the darkness is so resistant and why the light is not able to penetrate it? I don't think so.

You will immediately wonder what is wrong with the light. There is nothing wrong or out of the ordinary with the darkness. Even if you were to spend hours staring at the darkness, wondering how it got there in the first place and how it can possibly withstand the efforts of the light to shine, you would not get anywhere. Darkness is simply the absence of light. What you would need to do is find out what is wrong with the light. Is the light bulb covered in such a way that the light cannot escape? Is it burned out? Is there something wrong with the switch? Is there no power coming to the light? What is keeping the power from reaching the light bulb? Once you have figured out what is wrong with the light and have remedied the problem, the light will finally come on. You will see that the instant the light starts shining, the darkness disappears.

We look at all the evil and darkness in the world around us and wonder what is wrong with the darkness—why it seems to be getting darker and darker. There is nothing really different or wrong with the darkness. The reason it is getting darker is that the light is fading away. *The problem is with the light.* Why spend time and energy trying to figure out what is wrong with the darkness? We need to concentrate on finding out what is wrong with the light.

Whether the present darkness is the result of disobedience to parents, pornography, drug addiction, alcoholism, gambling, adultery, abortion, homosexuality, materialism, persecution of a religious group, or terrorism, they are all a direct result of the absence of light. It would be wrong to single out Muslims or other religious groups as the sole cause. The problem is with the light, with those who are supposed to be the light. Jesus said, "You are the light of the world…. Let your light shine before men, that they may see your good deeds and praise your Father in heaven" (Matthew 5:14–16).

Religious conflicts and wars will always be a part of our fallen world, but the darker the night is, the brighter our light should shine.

NOTES

INTRODUCTION
1. Aga Khan, "Tolerance a Religious Imperative," Ismaili Mail, http://ismail-imail.wordpress.com/2007/07/31/newsweeks-muslims-speak-out/.

CHAPTER ONE
1. Ted Ward, *Living Overseas* (New York: Free Press-MacMillan, 1984).

CHAPTER TWO
1. Phil Parshall, *Muslim Evangelism: Contemporary Approaches to Contextualization* (Portland, OR: Gabriel Publishing, 2003).
2. Jim Leffel, "Contextualization: Building Bridges to the Muslim Community," *Evangelical Missions Quarterly*, October (1998), www.emqonline.com/emq_article_read.php?ArticleID=2139-36k.
3. John Travis, "The C1 to C6 Spectrum: A Practical Tool for Defining Six Types of 'Christ-centered Communities' Found in the Muslim Context," *Evangelical Missions Quarterly*, October (1998): 407–408.

CHAPTER SIX
1. Ata G. Mikhael, *Islam in the Balance* (Detroit, MI: International Outreach Ministry, 2004), 4-5.
2. Mindy Belz, "Temperature Rising," *WORLD Magazine*, June 9, 2007, 42–43.

CHAPTER SEVEN
1. Mark Bergin, "Twin Visions," *WORLD Magazine*, May 5, 2007, 32–33.
2. New York State Education Department, "Chief Examiner's Manual for New York State GED Test Administration 2007-2008," 27, General Educational Development Testing Office, http://www.emsc.nysed.gov/ged/documents/exammanual6-08.pdf.
3. Queen Rania Al Abdullah, *Washington Post/Newsweek* "On Faith Series: Muslims Speak Out," Queen of Jordan Official Website, http://www.queenrania.jo/content/fromThePress.aspx?ModuleOrigID=artc&searchTitle=&yearFrom=0&monthFrom=&searchOrder=0&showMore=more&itemID=1912.

CHAPTER EIGHT

1. Ernest Hawn, *How to Respond—Muslims* (St. Louis, MO: Concordia Publishing, 1995).
2. Anne Cooper, comp., *Ishmael My Brother* (Kent, England: MARC Europe, 1993).

CHAPTER TEN

1. Walter Trobisch, *My Wife Made Me a Polygamist* (Downers Grove, IL: Inter-Varsity Press, 1971).
2. Walter Trobisch, *I Loved a Girl/ I Loved a Young Man* (San Francisco: Harper and Row, 1980).

BIBLIOGRAPHY

Aga Khan. "Tolerance a Religious Imperative." Ismaili Mail.
   http://ismailimail.wordpress.com/2007/07/31/newsweeks-muslims-
   speak-out/.

Al Abdullah, Queen Rania. *Washington Post/Newsweek,* "On Faith Series:
   Muslims Speak Out." Queen of Jordan Official Website.
   http://www.queenrania.jo/content/fromThePress.aspx?ModuleO-
   rigID=artc&searchTitle=&yearFrom=0&monthFrom=&searchOrde
   r=0&showMore=more&itemID=1912.

Belz, Mindy. "Temperature Rising." *WORLD Magazine*, June 9, 2007.

Bergin, Mark. "Twin Visions." *WORLD Magazine,* May 5, 2007.

Cooper, Ann, comp. *Ishmael My Brother*. Kent, England: MARC Europe,
   1993.

Hawn, Ernest. *How to Respond—Muslims.* St. Louis, MO: Concordia
   Publishing, 1995.

Krattenmaker, Tim. "How Little We Know About Religion." *USA Today*,
   April 30, 2007.

Leffel, Jim. "Contextualization: Building Bridges to the Muslim Community." *Evangelical Missions Quarterly*, October 1998, www.emqon-
   line.com/emq_article_read.php?ArticleID=2139-36k.

Mikhael, Ata G. *Islam in the Balance*. Detroit, MI: International Outreach
   Ministry, 2004.

New York State Education Department. "Chief Examiner's Manual for
   New York State GED Test Administration 2007-2008." General
   Educational Development Testing Office,
   http://www.emsc.nysed.gov/ged/documents/exammanual6-08.pdf.

Parshall, Phil. *Muslim Evangelism: Contemporary Approaches to Contextualization.* Portland, OR: Gabriel Publishing, 2003.

Travis, John. "The C1 to C6 Spectrum: A Practical Tool for Defining Six
   Types of 'Christ-centered Communities' Found in the Muslim Context." *Evangelical Missions Quarterly*, October 1998.

Trobisch, Walter. *I Loved a Girl/ I Loved a Young Man*, New York, NY:
   Harper and Row, 1980.

Trobisch, Walter. *My Wife Made Me a Polygamist*, Downers Grove, IL: Inter-Varsity Press, 1971.

Ward, Ted. *Living Overseas.* New York: Free Press-MacMillan, 1984.